——◄o►——

Robert G. Barnes, Sr.

1919–1996

This book is dedicated to my dad, who died while I was in the middle of writing it. He took the time to teach me many things about what it means to be a responsible adult. He never once fell back on the excuse that he couldn't teach because he never received any training himself. He just did it because he knew it was important to do. Thank you, Dad!

Ready *for* Responsibility

Ready *for* Responsibility

How to Equip Your Children for Work and Marriage

Dr. Bob Barnes

ZondervanPublishingHouse

Grand Rapids, Michigan

A Division of HarperCollinsPublishers

Ready for Responsibility
Copyright © 1997 by Robert Barnes

Requests for information should be addressed to:

🏭 ZondervanPublishingHouse
Grand Rapids, Michigan 49530

Library of Congress Cataloging-in-Publication Data

Barnes, Robert G., 1947–
    Ready for responsibility : how to equip your children for work and mar-
riage / Bob Barnes.
       p.   cm.
    ISBN: 0-310-20135-7 (softcover)
     1. Parent and child.   2. Parenting.   3. Interpersonal relations.
4. Responsibility.   I. Title.
HQ755.85.B36373 1997
649'.1—dc20   96-35876
                                             CIP

Interior design by Sherri L. Hoffman

Printed in the United States of America

96 97 98 99 00 01 02 03/❖ DH/ 10 9 8 7 6 5 4 3 2 1

CONTENTS

INTRODUCTION

In 1976 Alan graduated from high school with more awards than could be listed in the yearbook. More than anyone else in his senior class, anyway. He made great grades, lettered in two sports, played in the school band, and his senior year he was the star in the school play. It was no surprise to anyone, when they handed out the senior class superlatives, that Alan received the classification of "Most Likely to Succeed." What more could anyone ask for? His parents were very proud, certainly feeling that they had prepared him for his adult life. To all that observed his graduation, Alan seemed most likely to succeed at that adult world out there. Every area of training that his family and school had put before him, he had excelled at. The title "Most Likely to Succeed" seemed to be a perfect predictor for his future.

The surprise came at Alan's fifteenth high school reunion. The man who had been most likely to succeed, hadn't. Alan hadn't succeeded at any of the adult endeavors he had taken on. His marriage of six years was already over because he had repeatedly been unfaithful. Alan finished college, but he had been unable to find a permanent career path. Something he had never done in high school was to get involved in drugs of any kind. Now he was having struggles in this area. How could this have happened to a guy who was everything in high school? How is it possible that the person who was Most Likely to Succeed found his adult life so void of success?

Less than two decades after high school Alan found himself sitting in a counselor's office talking about all his dismal failures. Where were those successes? Alan had been well trained and groomed to succeed at all the activities that children and teenagers face. In those activities he did well. But these were not the lessons that prepare a person for the activities they will face in today's adult world. When he was confronted with adult responsibilities, he crumbled. He just didn't have the necessary skills.

Alan is not alone in his dilemma. Many of today's youth are receiving wonderful training for performing in an adolescent arena. But are they being trained and prepared to stand tall in the world of the adult? The adult world expects different behaviors and responses than does the adolescent world. More significantly, the adult world will be less forgiving and more tempting.

Are we really raising children who are most likely to succeed as they function as adults? Many good, well meaning parents are unknowingly setting their children up to fail. Many children are entering the adult world without the skills necessary to stay married. Without the disciplines to develop a career. Without the skills and understanding to make responsible decisions. Worse yet, many parents are sending their offspring out into the adult word without the slightest idea of what it means to be an adult.

It's a parent's job to establish a plan that will train a child in the skills he or she will need to be a responsible adult, rather than a forty-year-old adolescent. To send a child off without the necessary training is to put him in a position of being most likely NOT to succeed! It is our desire that this book will help parents establish a plan that will raise a child who will become an adult who is able to succeed at the most important challenges of life.

PART 1

Parenting for Tomorrow

Chapter One

———◄○►———

The Learner's Permit

Give her a credit card? You've got to be kidding! Why in the world are you doing that? She's only sixteen years old! She's still a kid!"

I was sitting at lunch telling a friend about our beginning of the year plans for my daughter, Torrey. Torrey was entering her junior year of high school and we were spending the summer making decisions about what we, as her parents, needed to be teaching her this year. We knew the school would be helping to prepare her for many of her academic challenges. The guidance department had been talking to her about college and preparing to take the SAT exams. School was also helping her in the area of poise and confidence via the drama department. They were even putting her in some debate situations, making her stand up for what she believes in. They had her write and present a paper on her views of abortion.

The school was working diligently at helping to prepare my daughter academically, but in what ways were her parents preparing her? If the school had thought it important to take some of the college entrance exams in tenth grade, just for practice, shouldn't I be setting her up to practice some of the more important things? But that brings up the real question my friend should have been asking at lunch that day. If the school was trying to prepare my daughter academically for her next step,

———◄○►———

No one can be expected to graduate from high school and simply walk into an adult world prepared. It takes practice.

———◄○►———

shouldn't her parents also have a plan in place to help prepare her for the adult world she would be facing?

Many evenings during the summer were spent getting ready for the new "practice opportunities" we were going to implement this year. It didn't seem to make sense to keep my daughter from practicing adult responsibilities before she left home. No one can be expected to graduate and simply walk into an adult world prepared. It takes practice.

The marines set aside time to prepare their soldiers. It's called "basic training" or "boot camp." The men and women in basic training don't practice the things they will have to learn to succeed in boot camp. Instead, they work on the skills they will need when they are out in the real world of the marine. They practice war games and battle simulations. That way they're prepared to do the things that are expected of them as marines.

Children need to practice the things they will need to be able to do as adults. I responded to my shocked friend at lunch. "She's going to have to learn about areas of adult life such as credit cards sometime. Shouldn't we teach her while she's still at home?" Regardless of my explanation, this friend looked totally bewildered. He absolutely couldn't believe that I was putting a credit card in a sixteen-year-old's hands. He had never thought of the teenage years as a time for adult preparation. Then I asked him a question.

"When did you first get a credit card or a checking account?"

"Oh, I remember that day well," my friend responded, looking off into space. "It was the last thing my dad did as he dropped me off at college. We checked into a dorm, walked around the campus, and then went downtown to a bank. He made the arrangements to open an account for me. He got me a credit card and a checking account, and then we went back to the campus. He and mom kissed me goodbye, and we all cried as they drove off. Then we cried again once a month as we discussed the way I handled my finances!" my friend finished with a laugh.

"What do you mean?" I asked.

"My dad and I argued every month about my credit card bills and my checking overdrafts. . . ." He stopped. Suddenly my friend stared off into space. I was having a hard time keeping a grin off my face.

He looked at me and said, "I wasn't even ready to handle finances when I was in college, let alone a junior in high school."

"You weren't ready because you had no training and no one to supervise you as you attempted this adult activity. Your parents just gave you the tools and said good-bye."

This was just the kind of thing I wanted Torrey to avoid. Just as the school sees it as part of their job to set up a practice opportunity with the SAT exams, it's a parent's job to set up practice opportunities with as many of the expected adult competencies as possible.

GIVE THEM A LEARNER'S PERMIT

It doesn't make sense to all of a sudden hand an eighteen-year-old a credit card or a checkbook and then drive away, leaving them without the privilege of daily supervision. What does make sense is to give them a "learner's permit" first.

Before you can drive a car alone, you must spend a period of time driving while being supervised. Ideally that's at least one year. It's a practice time. It's more than that, however. It's a practice time where someone is watching and giving on-the-spot input. If that's good to do before getting a driver's license, logically, it would be good to do for many other adult competencies. What's illogical is to turn our children loose in a dormitory full of other under-prepared eighteen-year-olds and then expect them to somehow learn many of the needed adult skills.

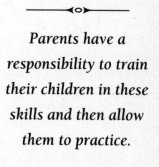

Parents have a responsibility to train their children in these skills and then allow them to practice.

I want to be sitting next to my child as she is learning to drive. That way I can advise her, help her make decisions, or even grab the wheel if need be. Slowly we can work our way out of a parking lot and up onto the highway. It's a gradual process needing much supervision.

There are other lessons of equal importance. Lessons such as handling money, handling relationships, making decisions, handling sexuality, disagreements, or responsibility, just to name a few. These areas of the adult world can have a life-changing impact, especially if a child is ill-prepared to face them. A young adult who enters the adult world without these competencies will likely struggle for the first decade of adulthood. How many times have we heard stories of people taking years to dig out from under maxed-out credit cards? How many tragic stories have we heard about young people being totally unprepared to accept the responsibilities of semester-long college term papers? So, they just flunk out. Worse yet are the stories about children from strong families getting away to a college campus and becoming sexually active because they had no training in the area of personal discipline. "But Mom," one pregnant coed said, crying, "he told me that he loved me, and I believed him!" Adult competencies take practice.

We have a well-defined learning plan when it comes to teaching a teenager how to drive a car. We take the time to practice the driving skills with our children, not because we push to teach this to our children, but because *they* push us. Children are very motivated to learn the adult behavior of driving a car. I gives them great independence. It also makes a statement that they are now entering into the adult world of responsibility.

What parents don't see, however, is just how much all the other needed adult competencies come into play when allowing a teenager to drive a car. There are financial responsibilities that go with operating a car properly. There is also a need for making responsible and safe decisions when driving. It's so much more than just operating a motor vehicle. It's a picture of just how well the child has been trained to act in an adult manner. A car can be a great means of transportation. Handled in an immature manner, however, it can also become a two-ton weapon. Operating a car doesn't take manual dexterity; it takes adult maturity. Parents have a responsibility to train their children in these skills and then allow them to practice.

FEARFUL PARENTING

"I hear what you're saying," my friend said at lunch. "But I just can't imagine giving my daughter Donna a credit card. It would be a disaster!"

"When are you going to do it?" I asked my friend.

He had no answer. Was he trying to protect his daughter from failing? He's only postponing potential failure until she's away from home when the mistakes can become even more damaging and habit forming. The people who will be advising her at that point will be other college students her own age, rather than her loving parents.

Why would parents wait to teach these skills? There is one advantage to waiting and letting a child learn while she's alone at college. If she's away her parents won't have to watch her fail. Who are they trying to protect?

There are some parents today who seem afraid to let their children practice handling adult behaviors such as finances, decision making, responsibility, or social independence such as dating. Instead of practice, they resort to isolation. They just keep them home and away from everyone else's "evil" child. One parent in church even asked me why I had my son signed up to play sports in the city league rather than the religious league. She couldn't understand why I would subject my teenager to the language and attitudes often heard and demonstrated during the games. When I responded that we were using this league not just for sports but also for practice at dealing with the real world, she was in shock. "Well, I was very surprised to hear that you are doing this, and I still say that I can't imagine why." Bewildered, she walked off.

This was a parent that did everything she could to isolate each of her children. These children rarely went to parties, even parties at the homes of other church members. As far as she was concerned, her children were just not going to be subjected to the "unacceptable behaviors" of other children.

Not only were her children not going to be subjected to these behaviors, but they weren't going to get to practice a response to them either. These children were growing up without being given any decisions or choices to make. Mom made all their decisions. Unfortunately, unless Mom either goes off to college with them or has them take a correspondence college course from their bedroom, they will be totally unprepared for life's decisions when they leave home. Assuming they are able to leave home.

PASSIVE PARENTING

There's another kind of parenting style. This second style we could call "passive parenting." Passive about taking on the responsibility of setting up a plan to teach the children the things they will need to know in order to be competent as adults. Unlike the fearful parent, who avoids teaching the child to make choices, this parent gives the child the checkbook without using any plan to teach the proper choices.

There are two passive parenting styles. The first one is based on ignorance. These parents don't understand that a child needs to go through a supervised learning process to learn how to make decisions. This parent is amazed that their child is rude, self-centered, and often sneaky but thinks that "that's just the way all kids are these days." When this parent catches the child in a lie, the parent asks the question, "What can a parent do with these kids today?"

That's the correct question, but the passive parent doesn't think that there is an answer. There certainly are things that can and need to be done. This parent operates without any plan. Rather than place choices in the child's path and then respond to the child's choices in a consistent manner, this passive parent gives in to the child's demands. One parent actually went so far as to say, "After all, she's doing so well with her grades at school. I feel bad telling her she can't have the things she wants. I guess I'm hoping that since she's such a good student, she'll be a good person and do the things she's supposed to do when I let her go to those rock concerts."

This particular parent has let the school do the work. The school has helped the child be a good student, but the passive parent wasn't doing his or her job. The parent wasn't seeing the great overwhelming need the child has to be trained to become not only a good student but a "good person" as well. Consequently we have an eleven-year-old going to inappropriate rock concerts because the parent doesn't understand the need to practice and teach the concept of choices. The parent didn't have a plan. The thought process seemed to be that if the child was proficient in one area, such as school, the child could handle freedom in the other areas as well, even though she was not prepared or even trained to handle the other areas of life.

The second kind of passive parenting style is motivated by defeat: "There's nothing I can do anyway, so why bother? If I told my eleven-year-old he couldn't go to that concert, he'd figure out a way to go anyway." The defeated parent has become passive out of sheer frustration. This parent has just given up completely.

When the child makes the statement " . . . but everybody gets to go but me," the parent gives in out of exhaustion. "I know he's doing all the wrong things! But what can you do?" becomes the motto of the defeated passive parent.

THE TRAINING PARENT

There is a plan that can be incorporated. There are choices that can and must be offered to the child. More importantly, however, there is a reason to train. There's a reason to place choices in a child's lap and help him learn to live with those choices. There's a reason not to isolate a child, but instead, give her practice opportunities at the decisions she will face in life. On the other hand, there's a reason not to just cut him loose or drop her off in life, acting as if there's nothing we parents can do.

The overwhelming reason for training our children is that they will have to go out into the adult world one day and make decisions that will affect the rest of their lives.

The overwhelming reason for training our children is that they will have to go out into the adult world one day and make decisions that will affect the rest of their lives. It's not the outside world we need to worry about. A parent's focus needs to be on the child's ability to make the best possible decisions concerning that outside world. Are we teaching them to focus on the bigger picture? Are we teaching delayed gratification? Are they learning how to properly handle material things? Without that training, material things will handle them when they are older!

Do they understand that there are absolutes, or are they learning to be motivated solely by the desires of the moment? Are they growing up with enough discipline to walk away from temptation or are they living for the next excitement?

NO MORE APPRENTICESHIP

"I don't remember my parents having a plan for what they needed to teach me, and I turned out okay," Alan blurted out while he was sitting in a parenting seminar. "I'm listening to the things that I know I should be teaching my son, and for the life of me, I can't understand why I haven't thought of this before. When did this get so hard?"

There were many statements in Alan's frustrated question. He didn't remember his parents having a plan for the process of child training. That's probably because they didn't.

Several generations ago, children were raised with a plan in mind. Parents knew that the children had to be raised and trained to go out and take on a specific adult task. Much of the time, that task was the family business. If the family owned a farm then the children were raised to know how to operate a farm. If the family owned a general store or a blacksmith shop, then the children were raised working around those specific areas.

Besides simply getting a job done, chores helped train children for certain adult tasks and taught the children responsibility and accountability.

The reason for this training was twofold. First, the parents needed the help of the children's extra hands when it came to getting the work done. Most families had five or six children, who supplied more hands for the job. Second, parents realized that one day they would be handing the business over to the children. It was very likely handed down from their parents. With that in mind, parents knew that there were many adult responsibilities that needed to be taught.

It was often an unofficial apprenticeship. At times the children were allowed to play and act like children, and then at other times they needed to take on adult responsibilities. This wasn't the result of mothers and fathers saying to each other, "You know, our kids are going to have to be competent in several adult behaviors. I think we should devise a plan that will help them learn" as much as it was that parents needed the extra hands to get the work done. Then as they found various areas of competencies in each of their children, they probably assigned them those tasks. These parents probably realized that someday they would retire to the "back forty," and the children would have to run the business. Not only run the business, but run it in a way that would allow them to take care of the needs of the parents when they retired. These two motivators were quite compelling.

Alan didn't remember his parents sitting around thinking about the training plan because the parents of the last generation didn't know why they needed to. In fact, many parents of this past generation operated under the credo, "I want my children to have what I didn't have," or "I want my children to have it better than I did." Many of our parents were the first parents who didn't want their children to work, because they didn't need them to work.

As our nation drifted away from the concept of the family-owned business, the day-to-day chores of the business were no longer required. Parents didn't even want their children to have to spend an inordinate amount of time doing chores, because they didn't have as many chores that needed to be done.

Parents didn't realize that their reasoning was faulty. Besides simply getting a job done, chores helped train children for certain adult tasks. This apprenticeship of chores taught the children responsibility and accountability. Lessons that seem to be in short supply today. Lessons that are very necessary if a child is to become a successful adult.

As time went on, we reached a point in parenthood where the system no longer automatically taught the children the concepts they would need when they became adults. Chores no longer needed to be done. Long-term projects for the children no longer existed. We are now teaching children how to succeed at childish behaviors such as school and sports, but not at adult competencies. The world of the family no longer automatically raises a child to succeed in the adult world.

WHAT DOES IT MEAN TO SUCCEED?

If we accept the challenge to adopt a training plan aimed at raising a successful adult we must first define *success*. Before we establish the plan we must define the goal. What is it to be successful?

Many would define success as attaining a certain quality of life. Politicians, in their quest to attract the electorate, talk of quality of life as having good health or a certain economic standard of living.

These particular definitions of *quality of life* or *success* leave many people out in the cold. If one has to be healthy or wealthy to be successful, then there are many who could never define their lives as such. I would certainly say that Joni Eareckson Tada has found success. Yet her success defies the popular definition. Her significant quality of life comes from her relationships with friends and family and from helping thousands of people with her conferences and radio program. Yet she remains paralyzed from the neck down and is not wealthy. On the contrary, I remember reading about a certain young man from the ghetto who dramatically changed his "quality of life" by becoming a television star. When he reached the top of the charts and was making many thousands of dollars a week for his television program, he killed himself. Quality of life or success cannot be defined by analyzing a person's health or finances. Success is far deeper than this.

> *A successful adult is someone who has been able to develop and maintain all three areas of life.*

My wife, Rosemary, grew up in a missionary family in a very rural part of Japan in the 1950s. Those were some of her happiest years, though the family had very little in the way of material things. But they were very close as a family, and they also knew that they were doing something that counted. They were missionaries, and they had the discipline and the drive to do what they were sent to do. That alone brought all of them great joy.

I would consider myself and my children a success if my children have the discipline and the drive to reach worthy goals as adults, if they develop the discernment to know when to do one thing and walk away from another. I would consider us successful if my children can handle and develop deep adult relationships, if they can maintain the discipline to work at a marriage relationship even when their needs aren't being met, if they can stay faithful to their spouses and to their dream.

Success isn't something that is inherited from a large estate or from healthy genes. Nor is it something that is won by means of physical giftedness. Success is something that is worked at and maintained.

A successful adult is someone who has been able to develop and maintain all three areas of life. That person would be happy and fulfilled in the direction his "public life" is going. Public life would include occupation and community involvement. A second and more important area of adult life would be the management of his "personal life." A person's personal life would include his family, extended family, church life, and other relationships. A person who is successful in his adult life is one who has been able to manage and develop his personal life. The most significant area of life is a person's "private life," who they are on the inside. Deep down inside his heart does he understand the bigger picture? Does he know that he is valuable and responsible to God?

This training for success in the adult world of occupation, relationships, and personal development all starts when children are young. The ability to become successful in these areas all starts with proper training. Training at a time and in a generation when the initial reason for the training is different. No longer do we need children to work on our farm. Today's parent must be motivated by the mandate. The mandate is found in the book written by a father named Solomon. In the Bible in Proverbs we are told to "Train a child in the way he should go, and when he is old he will not turn from it" (22:6). That is not an option, it is a mandate. If we parents don't take up the challenge to train the next generation of children to help make them most likely to succeed, chances are they won't. A lack of parenting leaves a child with severe consequences. For a child to be most likely to succeed, a parent must first decide to parent.

In the summer of 1995, a pastor of a very large church in St. Louis was doing exceedingly well in his work and ministry. His church was growing and his congregation loved him. His family life was also very rich and wholesome. This man's wife and children were all on his team. He was successful in two of the three areas of his life. The third area, his private life, however, was a disaster. Though he was a senior pastor, he still felt very alone and out of touch with God. The article in the newspaper described the man as a very hard worker, to the point of perfection. Though he had been taught how to work hard for God and help others, he didn't seem to know how to reach God for help for himself in his time of greatest emotional difficulty. This pastor was not a success in his private life, though nobody knew it until his suicide rocked the whole city.

Training a child to know how to become a successful adult has never been more difficult. Nor has it ever been more significant.

SUMMARY

1. Parents must decide to use a "learner's permit" approach to prepare their children for life.
2. Many parents are fearful of allowing their children to fail. Instead they just drop them off on a college campus without the necessary decision-making skills to succeed.
3. Other parents give up and adopt a defeatist attitude, feeling that there is nothing that can be done to help their children be personally disciplined anyway, so why try.
4. The training parent decides to set up an apprenticeship program to teach a child the things he or she will need to know to succeed in the adult world.

QUESTIONS

1. Before reading further in this book, think about some of the competencies your child will need when he or she becomes an adult.
2. What are some areas of personal discipline that you had to learn the hard way?
3. What are some of the areas of discipline that you still battle in your own life?
4. What are areas of conflict that you face in your marriage?
5. Could these be areas that you would like your child to be better able to handle as an adult?

Chapter Two

◄◦►

Children Are Growing Up to Be Children

It's a typical morning in the Johnson household. Mom and Dad have to get up early to get both kids out the door and themselves to work. Jack and Donna Johnson both know how nice it would be for the family to sit around the kitchen table and eat breakfast together, but that seems impossible. They think they have accomplished a major feat just getting everyone out the door with something in their stomachs. The last thing they do as they stand in the doorway before heading for their individual cars is review the evening schedule. They have to make sure that both of the children's practice schedules are covered.

As wild and chaotic as the mornings seem, the late afternoons and evenings are even crazier. Eight-year-old Billy and eleven-year-old Martha have each learned to get off the bus and go straight to the baby-sitter's house down the street. From there it's Mom's night to pick them up on her way home from work.

The next activity is homework at the kitchen table while Mom gets dinner ready. Soon Jack walks in the door from work and takes over the homework task while Donna finishes dinner. Donna and Martha eat while sitting in front of their favorite television program. Meanwhile, Jack drives Billy to soccer. They'll eat when they return.

In order to get the children to their activities each night, the parents must divide and conquer. Jack takes Billy to his soccer field in one part of town, while Donna drives Martha to gymnastics. Between 8:45 and 9:00 they rendezvous at home. Both kids get their showers, and fortunately it's one of those few nights when both children got their homework done before supper. With a story read to each child, Jack and Donna kiss them good night and walk out of their bedrooms exhausted.

A FALSE SENSE OF SUCCESS

The Johnsons are exhausted, but they also feel quite triumphant. Somehow they got everything done. Feeling like near-perfect parents, Jack and Donna all but high-five each other as they collapse together onto the couch. "Who else besides us could pull off nights like this with such perfect timing?" Jack asks as he loosens his tie for the first time that day. "We leave together in the morning, pick up the kids after work, get the school work done, get them to opposite ends of town for sports, and then deliver them back here and to bed almost on time. I don't know what we'd do without these cellular phones to coordinate everything."

"Yeah," Donna cut in while staring off wistfully. "Sometimes I feel more like a dispatcher than I do a parent. Do you think we're doing what we're supposed to be doing for our children?"

"How could you ask that?" Jack reacted as if threatened. "What more could we do? They're getting everything they need to grow up as happy, well-adjusted kids. Who do you know who does more for their kids than we do? When Billy and Martha grow up they're going to remember their childhood as a wonderful time, filled with lots of great activities."

Jack would have continued, but he noticed Donna wasn't listening. She had fallen asleep next to him on the couch.

There is a false sense of accomplishment bound up in this busy schedule: Keep the children busy at worthy activities; that's all a parent

> *There is a false sense of accomplishment bound up in a busy schedule: Keep the children involved in worthy activities; that's all a parent needs to do.*

needs to do. It is demanding, but how else does a parent keep a child out of trouble? The parental creed for this generation has been "Keep Them Busy and Keep Them HAPPY." But is that really what a child needs?

SUBCONTRACTING

Despite America's reputation for resourcefulness, this country hit a point where it no longer knew what to do with its children. For 150 years in this culture and for thousands of years in other cultures, the children were used in the family industry. They became helpers on the farm or in the general store. When the American culture left the family-owned business as a foundation of our economy and culture, we also walked away from a ready-made, well-organized parent/child training system. When the next generation didn't work for or with its parents anymore, the parents didn't know what to do with their children's unstructured time.

Resourcefulness seemed to win out. Sports programs, music programs, drama and dance programs, as well as many other activities became the main resource to solve this time dilemma for parents. Best of all, it seemed to fit the new mind-set: "I want my children to be able to have the opportunity to do all the things that I didn't get to do when I was their age."

The goal of individuality in our culture has enticed parents to look for ways of meeting the needs of their children, while meeting the parents' needs as well.

The goal of individuality in our culture enticed parents to look for ways of meeting the needs of their children, while meeting the parents' needs as well. After all, we all have the right to be fulfilled in our lives, don't we? If my children need wholesome activities in their lives, and someone else is willing to present these activities for the children, then we have the perfect solution. Find coaches and instructors to whom we can deliver the children. With the children receiving all the input they need, the parent can pursue his or her own fulfillment. Besides we're too busy to look into teaching things we never did, such as gymnastics and soccer.

Within barely a decade the American parent had become less a parent and more of a taxi driver, making sure that the children got to the proper subcontractor. It would then be the subcontractor's job description to teach things like soccer, baseball, gymnastics, piano, and so forth. The trick was to see to it that a child was able to partake of as many of these subcontracted activities as possible.

IT'S NOT THE ACTIVITY, IT'S THE ALIENATION

I was standing on the sideline of my younger child's soccer field. My son, Robey, was ten years old at the time, and we were watching him play in one of his last games of the season. While standing with several other dads, one of them asked me a question. "I'm curious Bob," he began. "Which baseball league did you sign Robey up for, Pembroke Pines or Cooper City?"

These are the two cities in south Florida that we live between, and each has a great sports program. In fact, parents here often pride themselves on getting their kid into just the right league. The problem was that in the aggressiveness of the baseball leagues to get in all the practices they possibly could, the baseball season overlapped the soccer season by three weeks. Kids were going to soccer on Tuesday and Thursday evenings and to baseball practice on Monday and Wednesday evenings.

I host a weekly radio program on the family in this community, and some people seem to think I have an inside track on certain activities. When my friend asked me which of the two baseball leagues Robey was playing in, several heads turned to hear my response. (I felt as if I were in an old E. F. Hutton commercial.) When I responded with "Neither," there was a momentary look of terror on the faces of these men. After a moment of silence I realized that I hadn't completely answered the question. Did my answer that I hadn't signed him up for either league mean there was a third league they had missed out on? Their attention to my response grew more intense.

"We're not doing a sport this season. I didn't sign Robey up for anything. This next season we're going to spend some more time at home." Their look of fear turned into one of disbelief. I could only imagine the many questions and thoughts that were now running through their activity-programmed minds: Could it be that Robey would go through a sports season without fleeing from the house each evening? Was it even okay to do that? Would the state welfare worker be visiting me for this "activity violation"? Would Robey get into trouble if he wasn't busy? How would this affect his future development?

The amazing thing was that staying home and being a family was an option that none of these professionals had thought of. Later that week I even received a call from one of those men who wanted to ask me questions about why I made that decision.

WE HAVE BECOME REACTORS TO THE FEEDING FRENZY

The "more is better" adage has come into play here. If special activities for my child can be good, then it stands to reason that even more of these activities would be better for my child. Activities have been offered in triplicate, and rather than thinking through them and making selections, the parents of America have reacted to them. It's a frenzy of reaction. I better sign up quick or it will get filled up before I've had time to think about it.

Robey and I once had field-level seats at a Miami Dolphins football game. The view of the game was horrible, but the opportunity to see the players up close was exciting. A line started to form behind me, heading through the double doors leading toward the interior of the stadium. It was almost halftime, so it wasn't hard to guess what was happening. Many of the other men who were sitting down on the field with their sons noticed the line, and they began to get in line as well. I said to Robey, "I'm going to go get in line before halftime to get us something to eat. Do you want a hot dog?"

By the time I got into the line to get through the doors it had grown to about forty or fifty people. Slowly we worked our way through the door, and on entering, I noticed people toward the front getting out of line empty-handed, with a disgruntled look on their face. Could they already be out of hot dogs? I wondered. Two more steps toward my destination and I realized the dilemma.

We had all seen people rushing for the line, so we felt compelled to take advantage of the opportunity. In fact, we even assumed that the opportunity was something we would want. In reality, it turned out to be a line to the men's room. We had gotten entranced by a momentary frenzy to follow the crowd before we even checked out where we were heading.

American parents have gotten involved in a frenzy to fill their children's afternoons, evenings, and weekends with "opportunities." There are wonderful opportunities to choose from, but choose we must. Parents cannot be caught in the frenzy that promotes the mistaken concept that more is better. "Look what a proficient parent I am. We're balancing all these out-of-the-house activities for little Billy. One day he'll be grateful for all these opportunities."

Parents must ask themselves several questions regarding the activities in which their children participate: What do all these activities actually accomplish for the children? What will these activities replace? How will they prepare the children for the adult decisions they will make during the next six decades?

These questions cannot be answered flippantly. Parents need to take time to evaluate the benefits of each of the activities their children are involved in.

SPORTS AND ACTIVITIES HAVE A PLACE

Sports are a wonderful part of a child's life. There are several character traits that can be enhanced by participating in a good sports program. Team sports, such as soccer, help to teach a child and young person how to work with others and sacrifice self-promotion for the sake of the team's needs. Working with a team helps prepare a child to learn how to work with others. It also affords a child the opportunity to learn how to make and maintain friends.

American parents have gotten involved in a frenzy to fill their children's afternoons, evenings, and weekends with "opportunities." There are wonderful opportunities to choose from, but choose we must.

Individual sports such as gymnastics or swimming allow a child to perform. Learning to deal with the stress and concentration necessary when performing alone are definitely character traits that will be utilized in the adult arenas of life.

All sports help to develop a child and young person's physical well-being. The physical and mental discipline necessary to excel in a sports program are very worthy lessons. Parents should take advantage, to some extent, of sports programs for their children. The mere opportunity to dive into a competitive atmosphere is very exciting and excellent training for a child's future. Learning how to handle competition is a very significant lesson, just as learning how to give forth every ounce of effort is a worthy exercise. Sports should not be dropped. Sports just need to be put in the proper time frame, as far as a child's future is concerned. The key here is balance. Many families have allowed sports programs to control their lives rather than the other way around.

Music, drama, and other non-sports activities also have a significant place in a child's development. They too teach discipline when a child practices to reach near perfection for a recital or performs under the stress of "the lights." This is to say nothing of the aesthetic value of learning appreciation for the arts and the work that goes into art.

These activities are relevant to a child's healthy development. They have great value. But activities outside the family should be seen for what they are—activities, not self-esteem enhancers or total program developers for a healthy productive adulthood. When compared to other things that a child will need to understand and experience before he becomes an adult, these activities play a far less important role than the amount of time that is afforded them.

Unfortunately, they often play a very disproportionate role in the development of an individual from child to adult. So much more needs to take place in the life of the child. These much-needed areas of development are lessons that a parent can and must teach the child.

WHAT DOES A CHILD NEED?

A child needs to understand the concept of relationship before he or she leaves home. Not just the idea of competitive relationships, such as are fostered in sports or even recitals. When we respond to life only as individuals trying to have our abilities displayed, we see every relationship as competitive. An understanding of relationships as competitive might be good for some areas of the business world, but this would be far too shallow and antagonistic for the most significant relationships such as the marriage. Yet we expect our children to grow up, get married, and stay married for all of their adult life.

Activities outside the family should be seen for what they are— activities, not self-esteem enhancers or total program developers for a healthy productive adulthood.

Children need to be taught the concept of blending. This concept teaches a child how to make sacrifices for the sake of the ones he loves, such as a spouse and children of his own. This sacrificial attitude is also necessary for citizenship and mature membership in a church. A childhood that is built around the precept of individuality rather than family will very likely produce an adult without any understanding of how to blend in a marriage. Rather than blend, he will expect and even demand that his spouse meet his needs.

Succeeding at employment means that a child will need to be taught how to work with and respond to authority. These are character qualities that take time to develop and can best be taught within the family construct. Even the schools we send our child to should not be expected to take on the task of teaching a child how to work hard and fall under authority. That's a parent's job. In fact, America is a nation with a shattered school system and we are trying to blame it on the educators. The fact that our schools are out of control is not so much a result of a faulty faculty, as it is faulty parenting. We cannot subcontract our children to academia and then blame the schools for our child's character flaws. The child's behavior at school is a direct result of the child's disciplinary training at home.

The disciplines of handling money, sexuality, and other outside influences cannot be taught by subcontractors. The home is the only place that can properly teach a philosophy of life that will encompass a plan to give a child a direct opportunity to practice handling these areas of outside influence. Soccer and piano alone won't provide a child with the skills needed to handle these influences throughout adulthood. Often young people have to waste their first decade as young adults "practicing" with these external influences. Having never had the opportunity or instruction to learn from their parents, they spend years wasting money, misunderstanding sex, and failing at employment.

The most significant area of character development necessary in a child's learning process is an overriding philosophy of life. Philosophy of life is the template that an individual uses to put over the top of every decision. The question needing to be asked is this: No matter how attractive or profitable this opportunity looks, does it fit with my personal philosophy of life? Even though I'm out of town and my wife would never know about this, how does doing this match up with my philosophy of life?

Children's activities and programs outside the home are less likely to teach a consistent philosophy of life than the home itself. A child needs to grow up with the opportunity to watch his parents or a parent live out a daily philosophy of life. Children learn not from lectures, but from lifestyle—not with their ears but with their eyes. They need to spend more time watching their parents than their coaches.

Take the Johnsons, for instance. They were very busy parents— they were busy, that is, running in several directions. They were pushing their son and daughter out of the house to activities, when in reality they needed to be spending more time as a family teaching a plan that will prepare their children for the adult world.

There's a great task that a parent must perform, and it encompasses more than seeing to it that the children are signed up for all the right activities. The task of training a child has never been more difficult. The changes in our society that have made it difficult came upon the parent before we had time to think about them. But that's no excuse. We still can't settle for training our children to grow up with only the skills that are necessary to be a good child. Each parent needs to adhere to a plan that will help turn children into adults who are able to reach their full potential. In other words, we need to think through the process of parenting rather than react to the opportunities for subcontracting.

SUMMARY

1. Today's parents have been led to feel successful simply because they have been able to juggle all their child's activities and programs.
2. In our effort to place opportunities into the child's life we have resorted to subcontracting. We have found other "experts" to teach our children the things we deem significant.
3. Constant activity away from the family only keeps the child from learning the most significant lessons of life.
4. Sports and other activities are good for a child, but they must not be used as a substitute for teaching life's most important lessons—lessons that will make a child marriageable and employable.

QUESTIONS

1. What extra-curricular activities are your children involved in?
2. About how much time do you spend getting them to and from these activities, including the time spent at the activities themselves?
3. What do each of these activities do for your child?

4. What do each of these activities replace?

5. How will each of these activities help prepare your children for the adult decisions they'll make over the next five or six decades?

6. Are you making good use of your children's childhood by keeping them busy with these particular activities?

Chapter Three

Sink or Swim?

For thousands of years, the parenting plan was pretty much the same. In fact, much of the necessary training was an automatic part of life. Parents needed their children to help with the work, so they trained them.

Seth was a typical boy of his time. His dad was a farmer who owned several hundred acres. Some of the land was used to graze livestock, and some was used to grow food for the livestock as well as for the family.

RESPONSIBILITY

When Seth was four, he was given his first real family responsibility. He was assigned the job of watching and playing with his baby brother. The baby was never out of his mother's or grandmother's vision for long, but Seth was the one responsible for sounding the alarm if the baby was about to do something dangerous, like chew on a rock.

At age six, Seth received a promotion within the family scheme of responsibilities. He was given the job of joining his father in the barn to help feed the animals each morning. He repeated this task with his dad each

For thousands of years, the parenting plan was pretty much the same. In fact, much of the necessary training was an automatic part of life. Parents needed their children to help with the work, so they trained them.

evening. Again, this six-year-old was never left alone in the barn. He was always somewhere within earshot of his dad in case he got trapped in a stall by one of the animals. But at the same time, Seth was learning more and more about how to take charge of the barn. He was just a few years away from being able to take on the daily care of the livestock himself. Seth's dad looked forward to that day.

The specific era of this scenario is unimportant. It could have been fifty years ago or a thousand years ago. The point is, in a society where the family operates a business, everyone becomes involved in that business. It could be a farm, such as in Seth's case, or it could be a grocery store, or it could be a hotel. In fact, it could be just about any service or business that existed up until a few generations ago. Whether it was the blacksmith, the cobbler, or even the bookkeeper, the children learned to help in the trade. Even the rehabilitated Ebenezer Scrooge in Dickens's *Christmas Carol* offered Bob Cratchit's oldest boy a bookkeeping job, assuming he would be following in his father's footsteps. Family businesses and trades were passed on. Children apprenticed adult behavior.

Spending time with a parent in the barn or in the family's store meant much more than just learning a vocation for life. It also meant that the child had an opportunity to watch a parent respond to life in general. When young Seth watched his father stay up all night trying to nurse a cow back to life, he got to see Dad work under stress. He got to hear his parent pray while doing everything humanly possible to save the animal. Seth learned a lot about dealing with life's difficulties during his day-to-day involvement at his parents' side. He wasn't required to deal with these stressful adult assignments, but he was present to see how they were handled.

He could also watch his father handle life's failures. No matter how hard Seth and his father tried that night, they couldn't save the cow. Seth could see how his father reacted to failing, and he could store this lesson away for future use.

The children of yesterday had the privilege of learning many things from the day-to-day activities that they shared with their parents. In fact, that closeness probably had an effect on the parents as well. They lived with the knowledge that they were being observed by the children. There's a tremendous accountability factor in my behavior when I know that my children are watching. Yesterday's storekeeper wasn't as likely to flirt with the clientele since he knew that his children were there watching and learning from his example.

OBSERVING THE FAILURES OF LIFE

It is as important for children to learn about failure as it is for them to learn about success. We don't realize just how much can be learned by watching a parent deal with something as intimate as a personal failure or difficulty. Sometimes we learned to make adjustments in our own life so we could avoid making the same mistake a parent made. But a more important lesson for a child to learn is that good can come out of failure. A failure might even start a person in a new and better direction. How do you overcome failure? Do you try again until you succeed? Try something new? Give up? It's more important for our children to see us struggling to find an answer than it is to merely tell them later that we did succeed. They need to learn the steps to take to overcome failure. For example, an adult exhibiting a willingness to continue to try again is sending a strong message to a child. That adult is offering hope. Children need to know that just because a failure takes place doesn't mean it's time to call it quits. No, it means it's time to evaluate, make corrections, and then try again. How are children to learn these skills if we aren't teaching them and modeling them?

> *It is as important for children to learn about failure as it is for them to learn about success.*

How many times did Alexander Graham Bell fail before he was successful at making the telephone work? What about Thomas Edison? He assigned teams of workers in his New Jersey workshops to solve problems systematically. It was as important for them to know what failed as it was for them to know what worked.

We are told that years ago a man retired only to realize, after getting his first retirement check, that he was in trouble. His monthly

—◄◦►—

Children need to know that just because a failure takes place doesn't mean it's time to call it quits. No, it means it's time to evaluate, make corrections, and then try again.

—◄◦►—

check was not going to be enough to live on. He evaluated this financial failure and decided that, in his old age, he would have to find a way to supplement his income. He had a special recipe that he believed he could sell to some restaurants. This man spent many months visiting over a thousand restaurants. All turned him down. Finally, one restaurant agreed to try the recipe Harland Sanders had for Kentucky Fried Chicken.

The backbone of this success story is not the special recipe. The key to his success is the fact that Harland Sanders knew how to deal with failure.

If yesterday's children had the privilege of being so close to their parents that they could observe an adult's response to one of life's great lessons—failure—what will today's children learn from watching their parents? Perhaps very little. Our children no longer spend that kind of learning time with us. They no longer see us responding to life's trials.

Robey was nine years old when he suffered what he considered a major defeat. His soccer team had made it to the city finals and there was no doubt in Robey's mind that they were going to win it all. Under the stadium lights, in front of packed bleachers, they lost the game. I took Robey out alone for a "man-to-man" dinner so we could talk. The entire meal he fought back the tears. Typical father that I am, I tried to tell him things like "It's only a game"; "there's still next year"; "all you can do is your best." Those words didn't help. Sure, they're clichés, and I know that they're true, but even I didn't buy in to what I was saying.

Then I said, "Robey, this loss may seem big now but—" Before I could finish he looked up at me and through his tears said, "You don't know, Daddy! You never lose anything!"

I couldn't believe he thought that. I could have easily gone through a whole list of recent failures for him—defeats at work, failures at home with a poor financial decision, many others. But he wasn't around to see me fail. And even if he was around, I didn't talk about it in front of him. I wanted to protect him from failure, even mine. As a result, as far as he was concerned, I just didn't lose.

I began to picture a child's view of life and the problems in life. A lot of what they know comes from television. But the tube deals out supposed answers to a contrived life problem within sixty minutes, with a few commercials thrown in. In fact, we're furious when they don't solve the dilemma in sixty minutes and instead flash the words "To Be Continued."

WOW! HOW COME I NEVER THOUGHT ABOUT THIS BEFORE?

A father sitting in the front of the audience for one of our parenting conferences said he was there because he wanted to be a good dad. All of a sudden he blurted out, "Wow! How come I never thought about this before now? I certainly have a lot of ground to make up! Where do we begin?"

He was ready to do something. But before we do something about the training of our children we must analyze our reasoning. "Do you really want him to learn the things he will need to learn before he leaves home?" I asked this father during a break. His wife had joined him and he responded with even stronger affirmation than before.

I asked them about long-term projects. Those who are successful in life are able to finish the long-distance races. Life rewards the discipline of the long-term perspective much more than the instant gratification it gives from something short-term. Both parents were nodding their heads in agreement. "But we can't think of anything long-term to put in his path. There's nothing like that for this generation." Chuckling, the man added, "What should I do, teach him these skills by buying him a cow and letting him raise it in the backyard?"

Parents often overlook the long-term projects that are right in front of our children. "Your son's in fifth grade. What about his science project?" I asked.

The mere mention of "science project" turned them off. "What a nightmare those projects are," the mother said.

FROM NIGHTMARE TO OPPORTUNITY

Often the things that seem to be the most difficult to get our children to do are the very things that could provide them with life's greatest lessons. Chores are a great example of hassles that could be turned into lessons for life. A science project is yet another one of those opportunities.

Using a science project as a teaching tool starts with answering two questions:

- Whose science project is this, anyway?
- Why does the school force these projects on us?

"Oh, it's his project," was one parent's response to question number one. She finished very appropriately with "But it seems to be mine to do!" The child's project, but the parent's job. That's actually the way we function too often when it comes to long-term opportunity.

Look at the typical scenario when the child comes home on a Friday afternoon. "Mom! My science project is due on Monday."

Mom, thinking she couldn't have heard him correctly, says, "Monday?"

It's the same scene that occurred the year before. Only last year, Mom vowed that this would never happen again. She even gave a speech: "I'm going to help you this year, but I will never do this again. If you fail to start early, like you're supposed to do, you're going to fail! I'm just not going to do it for you again!"

Actually Mom thought her little speech was all she needed to do. Unfortunately, her actions didn't correspond with her speech. Her fifth grader knew she would help.

The typical parent once again feels like a rescuer. Mother and son jump into the car and go to the store to buy the necessary items for the project. After all, a parent just can't let a child go to school empty-handed and have to explain to the teacher why the project isn't done. The parent knows how awful that would be. The problem is, the child hasn't yet learned that lesson.

The whole way to the store, Mom is asking the child for information on this year's project. It quickly becomes apparent that the child has no idea what the focal point of the project should be or even a topic for the project. Furious, Mom drives to the library so they can figure out what topic to do.

Friday night and Saturday are consumed with hurriedly putting the project together. Parent and child are no longer speaking a civil word to each other. Sunday, after a break for church, parent and child return to the kitchen table, which is covered with project materials. By ten o'clock that night, parent and child are both exhausted. In tears the child is sent to bed. "But Mom," he cries, "it's due tomorrow, and we haven't even typed it out yet!"

Those who are successful in life are able to finish the long-distance races. Life rewards the discipline of the long-term perspective much more than the instant gratification it gives from something short-term.

"You should have thought of that when you put it off till the last minute," was Mom's parting good-night comment.

But when the child wakes up the next morning, it appears as if some elf has magically worked the rest of the night. The project is complete. The information is typed out in four different fonts and glued perfectly on a board. It's all ready to go. The son is happy. The mom is pleased. Mom shows a little frustration when she has to call her son back to the house as he's leaving for the bus. He forgot to take the project.

Science fair night is an even better illustration of whose project this really is. The different projects are all on display in the cafetorium.

Kids are huddled in a corner playing with baseball cards. The moms are each standing dutifully by their particular project. After all, Mom is the only one in the family who can really explain it to anyone.

SHORT-TERM PARENTING

Even though we parents give lip service to the fact that we want our children to learn the important things in life, such as delayed gratification and long-term determination, we don't want to teach them. Rather than mark our calendars to help our children remember to prepare for the long-term projects, we end up rescuing them, with a bit of lecturing just before we start the rescue.

> *Even though we parents give lip service to the fact that we want our children to learn the important things in life, such as delayed gratification and long-term determination, we don't want to teach them.*

"What would you have a parent do?" is the question I get asked. "Should we just let them . . . fail?" That particular parent could hardly get the word out of her mouth. "I just couldn't do that," she said, sounding very loving. In other words, she loves her children too much to let them get bruised by failure.

Unfortunately that parent is just postponing the failure and the bruising. Her children won't fail as long as Mom is around to finish jobs for them. But when Mom is no longer there, and they're alone on a college campus or on a job, they'll fail. Failures at that level are much more significant and carry with them more severe consequences.

Parents must avoid such short-term parenting. Instead of thinking only for the day or week ahead, they should think for a lifetime. They should begin by at least thinking for a school year.

Whose project is it? That's one of the first questions a parent needs to answer. Perhaps that can better be answered after responding to the second question. Why does the school give our kids these projects to do anyway? Many parents will attempt to justify their aggressive involvement in things such as the child's projects by saying, "My child won't need to know about volcanoes anyway, so why not do it with him?"

A science project has to do with much more than science. It's an opportunity to help a child learn to set long-term goals. It's an opportunity to teach a child about delayed gratification. Sure, that child would rather put it off and do other things like watch television and play outside. But the project can be used to teach a child how to set goals and plan toward that end.

> *Parents may be taking the time to rescue their children from drowning, but they need to take the time to teach them how to swim instead.*

One father lamented, "You know, it irked me when my youngest borrowed money from me to be able to put a down payment on a new home and then the very next month took his wife to Colorado to ski for ten days."

What lesson had that man taught his son? To set some long-term goals and work toward them or to get what you want now? That son knew his father would be there to pick up the pieces. He knew his father would give him what he wanted. All this help being given under the guise of being loving parents!

Remember that loving parent who said she just couldn't let her child fail? She's the mother who finished her son's science project—for a second time. Her son believes that his parents will rescue him. He doesn't feel personally responsible. That's because his parents have taken on his responsibilities for him.

There are three options for this child's future. He could take a correspondence college program while at home so Mom can do his term papers. Perhaps Mom could move somewhere near the campus so she can keep tabs on his day-to-day paperwork. The third option is for the parents to just send him off to college. But don't redecorate his room. He'll be back. He'll be back because he won't be able to make it by himself. He's too irresponsible.

TEACH THEM TO AVOID DROWNING

Parents may be taking the time to rescue their children from drowning, but they need to take the time to teach them how to swim instead. We'd never throw our children out of a boat, knowing they couldn't swim. But that's exactly what too many parents are doing when it comes to life skills. Children are leaving home without the skills to cope in the adult world.

The most important thing for parents to do is to start preparing their children so they'll know how to swim when they get out on their own. Decide that it's mandatory, then develop a plan. Develop a plan before you develop a problem.

SUMMARY

1. Being in yesterday's family meant learning to be responsible.
2. One of life's great lessons is the proper response to failure. Yesterday's children got to see their parents responding to failure. Children today too often don't, and as a result, have no idea what to do when they fail.
3. Rather than constantly pulling your children out of water that's over their head, serve their needs better by teaching them to swim.
4. The parents' job is to love their children enough to let them fail, then teach them that failure is an opportunity to learn.

QUESTIONS

1. What are some of the skills that you believe are important for your child to be competent at before he or she leaves home?
2. How does your family life teach these skills?
3. What are some additional ways that these skills can become a part of your ongoing parenting plan?
4. Why does it seem so hard to teach these skills to our children?

Chapter Four

The Three Arenas of Life

As parents we need to decide what lessons our children will need to have mastered by the time they become adults. When they walk out of our homes, out from under our instruction, what competencies will be required of them? In other words, when the child comes off our eighteen-year assembly line, what should the finished product be able to do?

When a young man or woman enlists in the army, the first thing that takes place is seven weeks of preparation. It is understood that the new recruit is not ready to be assigned to any task until this period of preparation has taken place. It is also understood that Uncle Sam bears the responsibility to "parent" these young recruits and get them prepared.

I want my children to be prepared for the unforeseen, to be able to adapt to the unexpected. I want them to be able to think through the tough questions and end up with the right answers.

This is "boot camp." Many things happen in boot camp, but it is understood that the priority is preparation for the future. Boot camp instructors aren't focusing on how each recruit can become a great boot camp participant. They're not training for "today." Nor are they training them for sports and recreation. They're training recruits for their future. These recruits need to learn many things to become competent soldiers. And all these things they learn teach them how to survive.

Learning how to survive in the world is vital. The techniques can be learned. Remember the story of American fighter pilot Scott O'Grady? He was shot down in enemy territory in Bosnia. He was able to survive for six days in the forested wilderness subsisting on rations, insects, and grass for one reason and one reason only. He was prepared and trained for that possibility. His training had taught him how to do more than his primary assignment, which was to fly an airplane. His training had prepared him for the possibility of catastrophe. That training saved his life.

I want my children to be prepared for the unforeseen, to be able to adapt to the unexpected. I want them to be able to think through the tough questions and end up with the right answers. Their basic training needs to prepare them for the standard, everyday challenges of life as well as for the unforeseen crash landings. That means doing more than just signing them up for volleyball. Parents need a plan for basic training.

"But what do I do?" a panicked parent asked one day. "I believe everything you're saying, but how do I train them? How can parents possibly know what to prepare them for in this day and age?"

David, a friend of mine who has a hog farm in Illinois, is already working his plan. He told me that one evening he said to his thirteen-year-old son, Jeff, "I want you to stay home from school tomorrow and help me." This was very unusual. He had plenty of workers to help him on the farm. Besides, he never permitted Jeff to stay home from school for anything.

"What are we going to do, Dad?" Jeff had asked.

David said he wanted his son to know some of the more difficult jobs that have to be done with hogs, so he wanted Jeff to be there when the veterinarian arrived.

Jeff had expected to have to help out, but David told him that he just wanted him to be there. "Someday you might have to know how to do this, so I want you to see it firsthand now."

The lesson plan for our children's basic training should start early. The best place to start is to look at some of the areas of life that we have trouble dealing with. Ask yourself, "How can I help prepare my children to be able to make the best possible decisions about these areas when they are adults?"

How does a parent prepare a child for adulthood and the decisions that come with adulthood? When asked this question during a conference, one father blurted out that one of the most difficult tasks he has as an adult is to balance the work ethic he was raised with and his family life. "My job and my family seem to be in constant conflict!" he said. "The farmer you talk about was able to work his family life and work life together. I, on the other hand, find myself having to choose. To be quite honest, it seems easier for me to choose work. I find that I am more comfortable working long hours at the office than I am doing things with my family at home." He paused, then added, "And this is my second family. I don't want to keep making the same mistakes again."

THREE ARENAS OF ADULT LIFE

It is important for that teenage boy, growing up on a hog farm, to set foot in the barn on a regular basis. He needs to see how the various jobs are done. Better still, he ought to be doing jobs even though his hands might not be needed. His hands and his mind need to record the knowledge for later on in life.

It is equally important for our children to learn about the life they will one day walk into. We need to teach them how to function in the three basic arenas of life—public, family, and personal. Managed well, these areas can work in concert with each other. A person who doesn't know how to set priorities and blend the three areas of life can be tormented by a lifetime of conflict.

For simplicity's sake we label these three arenas your "public life," "personal life," and "private life." Each of these areas plays a very significant part in an adult's behavior and happiness.

Public Life

Public life can be defined as the role a man or a woman chooses for how he or she will function in society, mainly the working life. Some choose to work outside of the home, while others choose to work in the home. Some will choose, as their primary function, the raising of their children. Others see earning the income necessary for living as their main function.

We need to equip our children with the skills necessary for making an informed decision about their work life, weighing their aptitudes and preferences against job availability, location, and money.

People choose what to do occupationally as a result of what's going on in their private life and personal life or as a response to the culture they live in. An example of that would be the way people choose their life's profession. Some know (or have a pretty good idea) what they want to do. Others make their choice by listening to what people say about a particular profession. Some never choose; they just go to work at whatever job they can get. As parents, we need to realize that that, too, is a choice, but not a good one. Instead, we need to equip our children with the skills necessary for making an informed decision about their work life, weighing their aptitudes and preferences against job availability, location, and money. Some focus only on the money.

That's what Scott did. All through undergraduate school, Scott heard his fraternity brothers talk about their plans to make a lot of money after they became lawyers. Slowly Scott began to believe that his primary desire too was to make a significant amount of money. Maybe he didn't have to be rich, but very comfortable. No matter how many times his dad asked why he wanted to go to law school, Scott could come up with no better explanation than "I've got to choose something to do with my life. It might as well be something that will give me a good income."

After a decade and a half of practicing law, Scott had a lot of questions about his life. He was bored with law. He knew he shouldn't have been bored since he was what the world would call "successful" in his pursuit of wealth.

Paul, an attorney in his firm who had been in practice the same number of years, seemed much happier. Paul was one of the top producers, but he seemed to function differently than the other lawyers.

He had even turned down a big case that Scott would have done any-thing to get. And Paul's refusal hadn't hurt his standing in the firm. The boss had even invited him to play golf one afternoon last week.

Scott finally invited Paul to have lunch one day. He wanted to get to know Paul better and to find out whether he was really as happy as he seemed. Scott figured that Paul might be able to help him find out why he was so bored with his work, why the challenge and excite-ment were gone. The two lawyers' discussion went as follows:

"Why did you go into law?" Scott asked Paul.

"So I could help people," Paul said. "I know that sounds very idealistic but that was my original purpose. Sometimes I have to remind myself of that, but I'm still in it to help others."

"Not to make a lot of money? That's what my fraternity brothers always talked about—being a lawyer and raking in the dough."

"Oh, don't get me wrong," Paul responded. "I like making money, but that's not the ruling motive behind my decisions. I also work very hard at winning. You've seen me on the racquetball court. You know I'm very competitive. But more important to me than either of those is to make sure I always do what's right. I don't ever want to win a case and collect a big fee at the risk of losing my vision."

"Your vision? What's that?" Scott asked.

Paul hesitated, looking down at his plate, then up at Scott. "I make my decisions by filtering them through my philosophy of life. And my philosophy of life says nothing about making all the money I can. There's something else, and I've wanted to say it to you for a long time. It's not only my philosophy of life that comes into play. I also make sure that my family life is a priority in my decision-mak-ing process."

Scott started to squirm. The "family" was an area where he was already in trouble. He had missed numerous family events because he had to work or he was out of town or he was just too tired and didn't get home in time.

"Being lawyers allows us a little more control over our sched-ules," Paul said, ignoring Scott's obvious discomfort. "You notice that I'm not one of those guys who stays here at the office until ten o'clock each night. Do you remember two years ago when Mr. Benson offered me the big state fair carnival-ride case?"

"Yeah, why didn't you take it?" Scott asked, perking back up. "Nobody could believe that you gave it back. In fact, nobody could believe that Benson let you turn it down."

"It was hard. It was a great opportunity," Paul said. "There were times later when even I wondered if I had done the right thing. You saw how much press Grabill got while he was handling it. I heard he also got a big bonus. But did you also notice the damage it did to Grabill's marriage? And after winning that case, who did he take skiing? I understand it wasn't his wife."

"But tell me, why did you turn it down?" Scott asked.

"I'll admit, the offer was very tempting. I stayed up late two nights talking with my wife about what it would mean if I took the case—how much time it would take and how much money it would mean for us. We finally decided, together, that it just wasn't worth it. But believe me, turning that case down would have been impossible if I didn't have a plan for making those kinds of decisions.

"Here's my philosophy in a nutshell about making money. Who am I making all this money for, anyway? I can say that it's all for my wife and children, but is it really? If it is, then they must be my priority. But how could I say they're my priority if I'm never home? The financial and professional benefits of taking that case would have been tremendous, but at far too great a cost. My kids need me and so does my wife."

"Any regrets?" Scott asked.

"None," Paul immediately replied.

Scott told me he had suddenly been given a whole new way of thinking about his job—and his family. Before, he had been ruled by career opportunities and an office calendar. Can I change? he was now asking himself. Would a fast-paced firm like his allow him to change? Paul certainly was pulling it off. And Scott said he began to see that it was possible to change his way of thinking—about money, about his job, about his family—and realign his priorities. "Come to think of it," he told me, chuckling, "Mr. Benson just might ask me to join him for an afternoon of golf at his club."

Scott had never been taught how to handle the three arenas of adult life. Everything took a backseat to his professional life. That had always been primary. Now Paul had shown him a different way of looking at the responsibilities he had to his job and to the firm. Family was also important. Paul had made it clear that though he worked very hard at his professional life, he wasn't going to compromise his philosophy of life. And that meant that when there was a conflict between his family and his career, the family would be the dominant force.

Scott still had a lot of questions about all this: How does one maintain this balancing act? How does a person set priorities other than professional priorities? What is a "philosophy of life," as Paul had put it? How could he come up with his own? But most importantly, was it too late? Scott was afraid that too much damage had been done to save his family life. But he was willing to try.

If there is no plan, no philosophy of life, there can be nothing but conflict between the three primary areas of life.

We all need to understand that our public life extends beyond the occupation we choose. It extends to anything that pulls us away from the home. Generally, these aren't bad things; in fact, many are very worthwhile. The trick is knowing how to keep them from taking over too much of our life. Coaching sports teams, serving in a civic club, even working at church activities are all worthy endeavors, but they must be handled in a way that blends them with other, more significant areas of one's life. If there is no plan, no philosophy of life, there can be nothing but conflict between the three primary areas of life.

The pull of one's public life is very strong. Activities outside the home are easy to get caught up in. People tell us what to do and we do it. Immediate success. Often even public appreciation. We get our "strokes" that way. There is much applause when an adult succeeds in the public life. It's nice to hear children say, "Thanks, coach." It's gratifying to hear a pastor say, "We could never have done this without your leadership." It is very rewarding to be able to hand a high school senior a scholarship check made possible by money raised at the annual spaghetti dinner. We feel good; we go back for more. Home life is more difficult, and there's less opportunity for getting approval. We're taken for granted. We're criticized. We learn to avoid it.

Public activities are all worthy and important tasks of citizenship. Church participation is even a mandatory part of service to God. But God would never have us serve outside the home and lose our family in the process. I will never forget meeting with a twenty-year-old who had come back to church. His parents had long been stalwarts in the church, serving in almost every area. This young man had had a very troubled time during his teenage years.

Sitting at a restaurant with me, he said, "You don't know how hard it is to come back to church. I have spent so many years hating the church. I guess I felt like the church robbed me of my parents. No matter how much I wanted them to stay home and be with me, I felt like they were out doing church work almost every night of the week. I was very jealous of the church."

In his pain, that young man had learned the importance of balancing the demands between family and public life, a lesson he was now taking into his own life as an adult.

We all need our own philosophy of life. We need to know exactly what we believe. We need to set the priorities in our life, then make our decisions based on those principles. This kind of decision making is not something that comes easily. It takes time. It takes training. But if we fail to train our children, then we are training them to fail.

Personal Life

Personal life refers to one's personal relationships—a husband, a wife, our children, our parents—our family. We all make choices within the family, but sometimes they're not good choices. Sometimes we just can't decide what to do. To begin with, how does one handle and commit to a marriage? What does it really mean to be a parent? What are my responsibilities toward my own parents, now that I'm an adult?

All of these areas of personal life are learned behaviors. Unfortunately, too many adults were never given the answers to these questions. As a result, we are raising children who believe that the sole purpose of a family is to get their own personal needs met. They care not a whit for anyone else's needs. They're not willing to help out in the family. How then will they, as adults, deal with the give and take of marriage? They won't. We are no longer raising *marriageable children!*

> *We are raising children who believe that the sole purpose of a family is to get their own personal needs met.*

A marriage can either make two people miserable or bring them great joy. Understanding what it means to be married, to be committed to another person, is one of the main building blocks toward success in marriage, toward that joy. Little wonder that many of today's young people are choosing to stay single or merely to live with another person rather than commit to marriage. It's a commitment to another person's happiness that too many today are not prepared to make.

Private Life

The final and yet most significant arena of life is a person's private life, which covers whatever the person believes is the purpose of life.

I might go to church every week and if asked, "What makes you tick?" I would respond, "My faith in God is the ruling principle in my life." But is that true? Is that really the basis for all my decisions? When I talk about what it is that will make me happy, do I talk about a cabin in the mountains, a new boat? Other material things? It's not that those things are wrong to have, but if my children only hear me talk as if material things are the ultimate way to happiness, then I am leading them astray.

Children need to learn from their parents how to develop the private life that helps us make the difficult decisions of life, to do what's right. It's that part of our life that rules over our feelings as well as our desires. Either our appetites rule or we learn to rule our appetites. The pivotal word here is *learn*. Children learn from their parents, and this is a lesson that parents must teach their children if they are to succeed as adults.

CONFLICT OR CONCERT?

There's a simple test for determining whether we are properly managing these three areas of life. If the three are in conflict, with one demanding most of our time and energy, we flunk the test. These three arenas of life were not meant to be in conflict. They were meant to work together in concert to provide harmony in the lives of those we love. This working together, this harmony, is success. That's the message we need to give our children. These are the principles they need to understand before they become adults. This is the philosophy of life they must apply to have success in their public life, their career, and in their private life.

> *It's the parents' job to raise children who are able to be used by God to fulfill God's purpose for each child when that child reaches adulthood.*

It's the parents' job to raise an employable child. It's the parents' role to raise a marriageable child. And most importantly, it's the parents' job to raise children who are able to be used by God to fulfill God's purpose for each child when that child reaches adulthood.

It's a tremendous responsibility to be a parent. There are obviously some very significant lessons every child must learn before he or she leaves home. These are lessons that cannot be "subcontracted out." These are lessons for life that are best taught by parents.

SUMMARY

1. Setting an agenda for life is essential. Understanding priorities rather than just responding to demands is a major key to success in life.
2. Most people spend their lives controlled by their public life, the key component of which is their occupation.

3. A more important arena of an adult's life is the personal life, the key component of which is the family.

4. Everyone lives and makes decisions according to their private life, their philosophy of life. This is the foundation for all of our decisions. For some, that boils down to making more and more money. For others, who are seeking a deeper meaning and purpose to life, it boils down to where they put their faith and trust.

5. The handling of these three arenas of life (public, personal, and private) is the most significant lesson we can teach our children before they leave home. Either they will learn to balance these three areas, or they will be miserable adults crushed by the conflicts.

6. There are three questions to be answered by all parents:
   - Am I raising an employable child?
   - Am I raising a marriageable child?
   - Am I raising a child who will be able to understand God's purpose for his or her life?

QUESTIONS

1. What about you? Does it seem like your three arenas of life are in concert with each other or in conflict?
2. Which of the three arenas seems to be dominating the others?
3. How do you think that happened?
4. What can you do to turn this incorrect prioritizing around? What can you and your spouse do as a couple?

PART 2

❮◦❯

Raising an Employable Child

Chapter Five

The ICE Plan

It was the last game of Robey's soccer season, the highlight where the best players are picked for the game "under the lights." Robey was ten, worked hard, but was developing a little bit slower than other kids his age.

When we got to the game, we found that Robey would be starting as goalkeeper, one of the key positions. We were pleased but puzzled. On the bench were two kids who were definitely "all-county" material for goalkeeper, and neither was hurt.

At the party after the game, I learned the answer. "I was a little bit surprised to see Robey starting at goalkeeper tonight," I casually said to the coach. It was really not a statement, it was a question.

Turns out that Robey wasn't the best goalkeeper. The coach said there were two other boys who had more skill at playing goalkeeper, but they had "horrible attitudes. They throw temper tantrums when they don't get their way and ignore us when we call in to tell them to do something. They walk around like prima donnas."

The players the coach picked as starters for this final game had to have not only solid soccer skills but a record of working hard over the season. They had to have shown that they were willing to do what the coach asked. They had to listen and respond. They could disagree, but they had to disagree politely. And they had to hustle. It all came down to a willingness and an attitude.

That's it! Attitude. That's one of the keys to success. That's one of the keys to raising a child who is employable. Wouldn't it be nice if we could find a way to "bottle the spray" that makes one child a hard worker with a great attitude and hustle? Wouldn't it be nice if we could increase the chances that our child will be picked for the team as a child *and* as an adult?

EMPLOYABLE: MORE THAN SKILLS TRAINING

Being employable means much more than having the skills for the job. In fact, skills are something that you can, and generally must, teach an employee. More important is whether prospective employees have the right attitude. Are they receptive to the idea that they don't already know everything they will need to know? Are they teachable?

Over the last two decades of working at Sheridan House for Boys and Girls, I've found that one of the hardest assignments has little to do with the children who live in these homes. The hardest task at times is working with the brand-new college graduates who come on the staff. Right out of college, they are anxious to show us all that they have learned instead of letting us show them what they still need to learn.

> *In the world of business or ministry, there's very little room for excuses and "incompletes."*

We don't have time to follow around behind them to see that they accomplish each assignment. In college, they might have been graded according to whether the assignment was completed correctly and on time. In the real world, employers need to be able to go with the assumption that the job is not only done, but done correctly. We need A's every time. In the world of business or ministry, there's very little room for excuses and "incompletes."

Here's what your children's future employers would like you to ask yourself now:

- Am I raising children who are able to accept responsibility?
- If they don't know how to do a particular job, are they responsible enough to find out how to do it?
- Are they humble enough to ask for advice?
- Do they know that the team needs them to do their part?
- In short, have they been taught to understand the adult word *accountability*?

Accountability is no longer taught. Something else is being taught, and that is to blame someone else. You have an accident. Just find a reason or an excuse. Blame someone else. Even though you were driving too fast around that sharp curve and hit a tree, it's the county's fault for not making the road safe. There shouldn't have been a tree on that curve. The drunk driver who hits a car on his way home sues the bar for serving too many drinks. Or you can't be held accountable for your actions because you came from a dysfunctional family. Or you have a deficiency of some kind or a chronic syndrome. The list of excuses grows longer every day. There's a common thread. Each one is saying, "It's not my fault." And each person saying it comes to believe it.

Several years ago I read about a court case in California in which a woman was suing her employer for dismissing her. She was continually late for work so, after repeated warnings and discussions about her tardiness, the employer finally let her go. Her defense was the fact that she should not be held accountable for her tardiness because she suffers from a disorder called Chronic Sleep Syndrome. She just can't get out of bed in order to get to work on time.

Instead of being responsible enough to learn to fit the needs of the job, too many now ask others to bend to their needs. They rely on excuses to explain their irresponsibility. To say that they were never trained to accept responsibility and to be accountable is one explanation. Should we label it a Lack of Training Syndrome? Or are we giving them yet another excuse?

The point is, many people trying to enter the workforce are highly unemployable or at least unpromotable. How do we get out of this mess? By teaching our children responsibility at an early age. This lesson starts when a child is given specific responsibilities. Some still call them chores.

ACCOUNTABILITY STARTS WITH CHORES

"You know why I don't have my child take out the garbage?" a frustrated parent blurted out at a seminar on parenting. "It's just easier to do it myself. By the time I go through the hassle of having him take

—◄o►—

Chores aren't just to get something accomplished, though that's a real plus. Assigning a child regular ongoing chores is an opportunity to teach that child a sense of responsibility.

—◄o►—

out the garbage, and see to it that it's done, I could have done it myself . . . for the whole block!"

Why don't we assign chores for our children to do? Because we have forgotten the reason for chores in the first place. Chores aren't just to get something accomplished, though that's a real plus. Assigning a child regular ongoing chores is an opportunity to teach that child a sense of responsibility.

Parents today have become "time conscious" instead of "training conscious." They would rather do the task themselves than teach a child a much-needed lesson. It's easier, but that's short-term thinking. Parents have to stop counting minutes and start thinking about the needs of their children in the years to come. The phrase that every parent needs to write on their hand regularly is

I'd rather be able to say tomorrow, "I'm glad I did,"
Than have to say, "I wish I had."

Every child, in the long run, needs to be able to accept personal responsibility. It starts with those simple chores at home. Did you do it? On time? And correctly? It grows to the major decisions that have to be made ten, twenty, even forty years down the road. Parents know that's true. They know they can't cover for their children forever. But some parents won't let their children make a mistake, even a simple mistake. They don't see the value of making mistakes. They don't realize that we all learn from our mistakes. They don't trust their children to do anything on their own. And in that way, they're hobbling their children, keeping them from being able to fly out on their own, free and able to deal with whatever life has in store for them.

Twenty years from now, what will the parents of the ten-year-olds of today being say? "I'm glad I did" or "I wish I had"?

GARBAGE AND ICE GO TOGETHER

The need to take out the garbage regularly provides parents with a perfect opportunity to teach short-term responsibility on an ongoing basis. The task takes only a few minutes to complete, so it's clearly short-term. It's often smelly, which adds to the need for the child to keep it short-term. But it's more than that. Remembering to do the job every week is where ongoing responsibility comes in. Being nagged and reminded takes away points.

Parents today have become "time conscious" instead of "training conscious." They would rather do the task themselves than teach a child a much-needed lesson. It's easier, but that's short-term thinking.

So how does a parent teach these necessary skills of employment? With garbage. And without having to nag. Follow me.

Teaching responsibility starts with selecting a task that the child is able to do. Taking out the garbage is a natural. I say this because children in America today are being short-changed by parents who have very low expectations of what their children can do. Or perhaps the children have all gotten together and devised a plot to convince parents that they are incapable of household responsibilities. Either way, garbage remains a natural. The smell can be a silent reminder. An advantage for the child.

ICE

Life on the farm gave a parent a ready-made plan for teaching responsibility. The eggs needed to be collected each morning, so someone taught the children how to do it. Today's home has garbage to teach responsibility. But first, parents must see a need to put the responsibility for transporting the garbage on the child's shoulders. The parents' plan then must devise a way for the child to pick up and run with the responsibility on their own. We use a method called the ICE plan.

The *I* of ICE stands for Instruction. This first step is the parent's responsibility. The parent must think through and then instruct the child about the chore the child is about to become responsible for.

The second step is *C* for the Consequence. This is a shared responsibility. The parent thinks of and presents to the child the consequence to be meted out if the responsibility is not accepted by the child and the job is not done. The child's part is to either accept the responsibility and do the job or "pay" the consequence. Here is the greatest area of argument and the danger (if a parent fails to handle this properly) of the child carrying into adulthood the belief that there is justification for irresponsible behavior. Namely, the "It's not my fault!" syndrome.

> *Children in America today are being shortchanged by parents who have very low expectations of what their children can do.*

The third step is *E* for the Experience portion of the learning process. Children must be given the opportunity to exercise their options. They must be allowed to choose what they will do.

Instruction

Once the proper chore has been selected (it's still garbage), it needs to be explained to the child. That's the *I* in the ICE plan for teaching responsibility: Instruction.

The summer before Robey started kindergarten, we introduced him to his new chore of taking out the garbage. We traditionally used the summer months to teach chores we expected our children to be responsible for during the next school year.

"Robey," I began, "from now on one of your family chores is going to be to take out the garbage." We made it a big event by going to the local hardware store together and purchasing two new garbage cans on wheels. We also purchased a new box of big, black trash bags.

After talking the whole way home about never putting one of those trash bags over his head, I continued in the kitchen with the instruction portion of the lesson on responsibility. "The garbage man comes every Wednesday and Saturday mornings. The best time to take the garbage out is the night before those days. Since this is Tuesday night, I'm going to show you how to do this job. Follow me and watch how I empty the wastebaskets in every room into this big, black garbage bag that I drag from room to room. See how I put a new liner in each wastebasket so it'll be ready for the next time? Friday night we'll switch and I'll follow you around, as you do it, so that we can make sure you're doing it right. After that, it will be up to you."

As we worked, I kept up the instruction. "After next week, I'm not going to be reminding you about this job. Next week, when you're doing this by yourself, I'll remind you on Tuesday and Friday night. After that you're on your own to remember."

I could tell he was seeing a problem when he said, "How will I remember if you don't remind me?"

"Robey, that's part of the lesson. It's important for you to find a way to remember to do this. You might want to put a sign on your door or on the bulletin board to help you remember that Tuesday and Friday nights are garbage nights. Learning to remember is a more important part of this job than taking out the garbage. I'm not trying to teach you to be a good garbage man. I'm trying to help you learn how to be responsible enough to remember to do your chores. The most important part of this chore is to remember to do it without being told."

Consequence

His second question told me where his thinking had taken him. "Daddy, what happens if I do forget to take out the garbage?"

One of the things many parents fail to do when teaching responsibility is to think of the consequence ahead of time. Before the child is even given the instructions for the responsibility being assigned, the parent needs to have thought through the consequence for a task not completed as assigned. Because, most likely, it's not going to be

Before the child is even given the instructions for the responsibility being assigned, the parent needs to have thought through the consequence for a task not completed as assigned.

completed as assigned. Your child has to know what's going to happen. And the child won't go so much by what you say, but by how you follow through with the consequence.

I had carefully thought this through. "If by seven o'clock on Wednesday or Saturday morning, you haven't taken the garbage out yet, I'm not going to yell or scream at you. I'm just going to take the garbage out myself. Once it's 7:00 A.M. and you see me going through the house collecting the garbage, it's too late. Don't try to run up to me and say, 'I'll do it from here, Daddy.' It will be too late. I'm going to do your job.

"On those days when I have to take the garbage out because you forgot, when you get home from school and the garbage cans are empty, you will have to get the hose and the brush with the long handle and wash out the garbage cans."

"Oh, that's gross!" He made a face. "I don't want to have to clean out those garbage cans!"

"You misunderstood me," I responded. "You won't ever have to wash out the garbage cans. Just take out the garbage on time. But the days you don't take it out, you'll have to wash the garbage cans. There's a real easy way to avoid having to wash them out. What is it, Robey?"

"I know," he said, lowering his voice. "Don't forget to take out the garbage."

The consequence for failing to accept a responsibility must be explained to the child. That way the child begins to understand the concept of accountability. If you fail to do something you're supposed to do, you *will* be held accountable. It's not the garbage or the completion of any other chore that's important. It's the fact that our children must enter adulthood able to take on responsibility and be accountable.

The parents who miss the point of this lesson will soon allow the chore to fall by the wayside. These are the same parents who gave up teaching their children chores because it was easier to do the jobs themselves. Those children will grow up without the training they need to take on life's responsibilities.

Remember, it's not the chore that's important. It's the concept. We're training the concept of responsibility with "garbage."

Experience

The third component of the ICE plan, the experience, will be the most difficult. In fact, it's the step that causes both parents and children to falter, so be careful. Parents need to step back and allow their children to experience the consequences of their behavior. And remember, no rescue efforts. Whatever happens is the result of the child's behavior.

Back to Robey. If he takes the garbage out, that's it, no washing out the garbage cans. If he doesn't, he'll be scrubbing out the garbage cans. For many weeks, we had a ritual of Robey washing out trash cans on Wednesday and Saturday afternoons. We must have had the cleanest trash cans in all of south Florida. Robey was too short to be able to stand over the cans and stick the long-handled scrub brush in, so he had to put the cans on their side, up against the house, and wash them out. Whenever possible, he would look up at me through big tears, trying to place the blame for this horrible situation on me.

Many times, as the weeks rolled by, I wanted to say, "Robey, do you know what day it is today?" I just couldn't stand it. I wanted him to win at this task so badly. I wanted to help him by reminding him to get the chore done. But then it would have become my responsibility, not his. I'd have been using little more than his body to get the job done, certainly not his brain. And he wouldn't have learned, by remembering on his own, the concept of responsibility.

I had to allow him to win or fail on his own. We had to both go through the growing pains as he slowly learned how to remember his job. When he didn't remember or chose not to remember, he was held accountable.

Allowing a child an opportunity to fail is extremely important. The parent who keeps rescuing a child from failure is robbing the child of two things—the taste of true victory and the future that could have been possible.

Without having the training and the opportunity to learn how to stand on his own two feet, how to overcome failure, a child enters adulthood afraid to risk doing great things. Having never dealt with and overcome failure, that adult will be afraid to risk, afraid to go beyond the ordinary, still afraid to fail or even make a mistake. In short, the parents who keep bailing out their children relegate them to live as followers rather than as leaders. They have robbed their children of opportunities. Leaders have learned how to stay focused on the goal, regardless of the number of failures encountered along the way.

Inspect What You Expect

The final step in teaching responsibility is to *inspect* what we expect our children to do. Not to do so is irresponsible on the parent's part. Children need to know how they've done. Take the time to hold your child accountable by inspecting the chore and following through with the proper response. That's the completion of the plan.

The saying to keep us on track is "Twenty years from now, I'd rather be able to say, 'I'm glad I did,' than 'I wish I had.'"

SUMMARY

1. The first step toward raising an employable adult is to teach the child the concept of personal responsibility. That starts with giving them chores.
2. Select a chore and then utilize the ICE plan:
   - Instruction
   - Consequence
   - Experience
3. Make sure you are willing to inspect what you expect. Hold your child accountable.
4. Twenty years from now you want to be able to say, "I'm glad I did," rather than "I wish I had!"

QUESTIONS

1. What chore can you select that will teach your child the concept of short-term responsibility?
2. How will you go through the instruction part of this process?
3. What will the consequence be for not accepting this responsibility?
4. When can you begin?

Chapter Six

——◦——

Avoid Irresponsibility and Excuses

Responsible people don't give excuses." I heard it over and over in the weekly staff meetings at my first job, when someone was trying to explain why he had dropped the ball on some assignment. And the boss always continued with "Either they got the job done on time and didn't need an excuse, or they accept the consequences without excuse." You only had to hear it once. After that, you chose to get the job done.

——◦——

Responsible people don't give excuses.

——◦——

This was a boss who had already completed a very successful career in the military. If he did one thing for everyone who worked for him, it was to make us all very responsible. So responsible that other managers were constantly trying to steal people from his division. His people learned to be responsible employees.

"But Daddy," was how my third-grade daughter introduced her excuse. "I forgot."

"It seems to me, Torrey, that you have forgotten your spelling book three other times this week," I said on one such occasion. "Why do you think that happens?"

"Because I start talking to my friends and I forget," Torrey explained. "Spelling is at the beginning of the day and by the time we start to pack our backpacks to go to car pool, I forget."

Do you hear it? This excuse was great. It was well thought out as it cast the blame for her forgetting the spelling book back on the school. After all, if they hadn't put her spelling class at the beginning of the school day she would be able to bring the spelling book home each afternoon. It was really the school's fault for putting so much time between the spelling class and the moment she would need to pack the book. She almost had me.

THE PLEASER VERSUS THE BARBARIAN

Most children fall into two general classes: Pleasers and Barbarians. Pleasers really mean to get the job done, but they forget. Once they're placed into a plan such as the ICE plan, they will be able to learn to accept responsibility very quickly. They want to please.

Barbarians, on the other hand, are not so easy. Barbarians will either forget or just plain choose not to do the task at hand. Not only will the task not get done, but Barbarians are prepared with the perfectly logical reason that the task wasn't done. Barbarians just want to win. More than anything they want to win the argument that the irresponsible behavior is really not their fault. Of course it's not!

Barbarians are prepared from birth with imbedded assistance that they use to justify their irresponsibility. They carry with them a special tiny "excuse card" that can only be seen by them. When it comes time to debate the issue as to where the responsibility falls, they pull out the card of excuses and go down the list. Don't look for it; parents can't see it! You won't have to see it, you'll just hear a remarkable list of excuses:

I'm grateful I live in the country I live in and am able to feed and educate my children. No, I don't think "fair" is an issue that I want to spend a lot of time on. As an adult I have come to know that to make things fair I'd have to give back a lot.

"You didn't tell me that!"

"I forgot! Didn't you ever forget?"

"This is just the first time! If you give me one more chance I know I can do it!"

Then comes the final excuse on the card. This excuse paralyzes most parents. When the child says it, the parent stops in his tracks. "It's not fair!" For some reason, that particular excuse makes a parent sit down and think, "Well, maybe he's right. Maybe this isn't fair. And I want to make sure I'm being fair in my dealings with my child."

Let's talk about "fair." What is fair in the adult world that they will be traveling in? Is it fair that one woman has breast cancer and another doesn't? Is it fair when one person loses a child and others don't? Did fairness come into play when the day-care center in Oklahoma City was blown up and some parents lost their babies while others didn't? I don't think "fair" is an issue to respond to. Of course life's not fair. In fact, if you're able to purchase and read this book, you certainly have more than your share of "fair." The majority of people in the world don't have the resources or opportunity to purchase a book. If we think about it in light of what we see in the news each night, we are certainly in a position to say that we are more than blessed. I don't think I even want "fair." I'm grateful I live in the country I live in and am able to feed and educate my children. No, I don't think fair is an issue that I want to spend a lot of time on. As an adult I have come to know that to make things fair I'd have to give back a lot. I want my children to learn that they are blessed as they grow up, rather than spend time complaining about whether various circumstances are fair or not.

A child needs to learn that it is his irresponsibility that is actually "unfair." In a plan such as the ICE plan, a child needs to know that he has chosen a consequence by his lack of responsibility. That is what is fair. Not his complaint. In fact, it's not fair that he is complaining about the results of his irresponsibility. He knew ahead of time what the results would be. What's fair is that he should accept the consequences for his behavior.

Each of your children will respond differently. Your Pleaser might not spend a lot of time on the fairness issue. The ICE plan will be easier for him.

Your Barbarian, on the other hand, will quest after the win. He will want to win the argument regardless of the responsibility. He's practicing for law school. The ICE plan will be more difficult to enforce, but it is so important to implement it and use it consistently. We need to place the Pleaser and the Barbarian in the plan and prepare for their different responses. One will learn quickly, while the other will spend time testing his parents' commitment and resolve to stay with the plan of teaching responsible behavior.

BEATING THE EXCUSES

Torrey was brilliant at being able to come up with excuses as to why she had been unable to bring home her spelling book. They all sounded very reasonable at first. But after I thought about it, twenty years from now I didn't want to hear her boss or spouse say, "Torrey has a great mind, but when it gets right down to it, she just doesn't follow through and get the job done. I get tired of hearing all her excuses!"

"Torrey, I think that the mistake has been mine," I began, as she stared up at me with a look of disbelief. "I've made a mistake by arguing with you about this. I don't want to do that anymore (as if that was going to stop her from arguing). From now on we're going to use a new plan."

Instruction

"Tomorrow, when I pick you up from school, you must have your spelling book with you. If not, we're going to pull over and go in and get it." That afternoon we got her book and went over to my office to make a photocopy of all forty-eight pages of the book.

"Oh, this is great, Daddy," Torrey said, as we were copying the book. "This means we'll have an extra copy. I won't have to remember to bring it home anymore."

That sounds very logical. It would also be temporarily helpful to have a home spelling book as well as a school spelling book. But that's not the issue here. The issue is not the fact that we have too few spelling books and want the luxury of having an extra book. That would be a very shortsighted response to this situation, a response of parental convenience rather than parental responsibility. The issue was the fact that this was an opportunity to teach a much-needed adult behavior called responsibility.

Consequence

"No, Torrey," was my response to her statement about now having two spelling books. "I want you to find a way to remember to bring your school spelling book home every single day until the end of this month. On the days that you don't bring the spelling book home I will take out my spare copy and you will use it to write every one of this week's words ten times each."

"Ten times each!" she all but passed out from shock. "My teacher never makes me write the words ten times each. For homework we only have to write them five times."

"No you misunderstand me," I cut into her tears of protest. "You might never have to write the words ten times each. Just decide to remember to bring the book home. The days you choose not to bring the book home are the only days you'll have to write the words ten times each."

"I don't choose to forget my book," she said in protest. "I just forget. I can't remember. Spelling is so early in the morning. It's not my fault that I can't remember."

"Let me ask you something," I said concentrating on remaining calm. "If I gave you a one-hundred dollar bill at breakfast and said, 'Keep this with you, and if you can show it to me at dinner, you can have it.' Do you think you'd forget to show it to me at dinner?"

"That's not the same." She continued her protest.

"Sure it's the same," I responded. "The one-hundred dollar bill would become very important for you to remember, so you would concentrate on doing what you needed to do to complete the job of showing it to me. I'm trying to make bringing home your spelling book something you choose to remember to do. The only way I know how to do that is to use this extra book. But you will be the one choosing to write the words ten times each, not me. Just choose to remember to bring the book home."

End the Debate

The Barbarians in most homes will argue just for the sake of arguing. In a parent's attempt to be "fair," the adult can often find herself explaining the same things over and over, thus putting the child in the control seat. Once the questions have been answered, and it is obvious that the child is continuing to debate by asking the same questions or protesting repeatedly, it's time to show leadership.

Once the questions have been answered, and it is obvious that the child is continuing to debate by asking the same questions or protesting repeatedly, it's time to show leadership.

I love the bumper sticker that says, " . . . because I'm the mommy! That's why." There comes a point where we can actually teach a child that it pays to argue. When we permit her to continually delay or derail the process by arguing, asking the same questions repeatedly, or complaining, we facilitate the excuse mentality. That carries into adulthood. Your child's spouse or boss will get really tired of this ongoing tactic of debating rather than producing.

Listen. Then decide when to say that enough discussion is enough. It is important to listen, however. I do want to teach my children to ask questions. I don't want to teach my children to be intimidated by authority. Instead, I want to teach them to choose to be respectful of the positions of authority. Allow questions until they become games or excuses. Then it's time to get to work.

Review the Plan

"So now you know what you are supposed to do. You're going to remember to bring the book home every night for the rest of this month. That's every night whether you have spelling homework or not."

Often, in the heat of the debate, the child can actually forget the main points of the plan. Another thing can also take place. There might be moments where the parent has become so confused that the parent can't remember what the final plan was. It's important to make sure everybody is on the "same page." Burt and Louise were parents who found it best to write the plan down. They set up a form with a large "I" on top and wrote out the instructions. Then under a large "C" they wrote out the consequences. That way they could refer back to it or point their son Michael back to it when it came time to deal with the irresponsible behavior.

> *Whatever it takes, it is important for the parent to be confident that both parent and child understand the plan.*

Whatever it takes, it is important for the parent to be confident that both parent and child understand the plan. If the parent is the least bit hazy on the plan, when it comes time to follow through on the consequence, the child will be sure to work hard at making the parent believe that "You never said that!" or "I thought you said . . ." or "Yes, but the last thing you said was . . ." Review the plan to make sure both parent and child have the same understanding.

EXPERIENCE

When it comes to teaching responsibility, there are some opportunities that have a lot of "gray area." Situations when a parent really can't be sure if the child's irresponsibility caused him to forget or if it was truly someone else's error. But other times, even when a child is smart enough to try to pass the buck, it is obvious where the responsibility lies. The spelling book opportunity was one of those times when the sole responsibility was on Torrey's shoulders. It was an opportunity to teach the concept of "no-excuse responsibility" that could not be passed up. In fact, only irresponsible parents would not take advantage of teaching their child this much-needed adult skill.

Torrey didn't learn the lesson right away. She's too smart for that. She first had to decide whether her parents were committed to this plan of teaching her to be responsible rather than thinking up excuses at the last minute. She wrote a lot of spelling words in tears, trying to give reasons why she forgot to bring the book home. She also told us that we weren't being fair. That if we loved her, we'd just let her use her extra book that was here at home. Over and over, we had to tell her that it was because we loved her that we stayed with the plan.

A STEP TOWARD ACCOUNTABILITY

We spent weeks of coming home to face a little girl who had forgotten her spelling book. We listened to creative, in fact, brilliantly put together excuses when we would ask for Torrey's spelling book. We would hear things like, "I put it in there. I don't know what happened to it." Then we would go through the arguments about writing the words. Finally we hit a high point of responsibility. It wasn't so much that she had accepted the responsibility, as it was that she accepted the accountability.

I came home from work one evening and Torrey was already at the kitchen table finishing up writing each of her words ten times each. She had forgotten the book, but she had accepted the responsibility for being accountable for her actions. Though she wasn't happy about doing it, she was becoming accountable enough to do the job without an argument. In fact, that night she did it before she was even asked about the book. That's significantly more than half the battle. In the adult world of relationships, whether in employment or in marriage, few things are more important to conflict resolution than a willingness to admit fault. Many minor adult issues become major

> *In the adult world of relationships, whether in employment or in marriage, few things are more important to conflict resolution than a willingness to admit fault.*

conflicts because one of the two involved will not accept the responsibility for his or her behavior.

This was a great step. Even though Torrey had not reached the place of choosing to remember the specific responsibility, she was choosing not to give excuses. She was choosing to be held accountable.

THE DAY OF REJOICING

There were days when Torrey would bring her spelling book home and we made a big deal about it. No day was bigger, however, than the day when she had brought the spelling book home for the fifth day in a row. Rosemary called me at the office to let me know that Torrey had indeed brought her spelling book home and that this was her fifth day. Actually, Rosemary was reminding me so that I wouldn't come home and miss a big opportunity.

This was a triumph, the acceptance of responsibility, and I wanted to respond in a big way. Some parents would say at this point, "Isn't the reward the fact that she didn't have to write her spelling words over ten times each? Why should you do more than that? After all, she just did what she was supposed to do. If we're training her to be able to respond to the adult world, isn't an extra reward teaching her to expect something that won't happen in the world of employment? Her boss isn't going to do that."

Actually a good boss just might do that with something like a plaque or label. Many people have received the honor of salesperson of the month or most improved something-or-other. But we still must remember that though we are training the child to become a responsible adult, we are still dealing with a child. Yes, there will be consistent consequences for irresponsible behavior, but there should also be fun rewards for effort. It's the obvious effort that is being rewarded. For a child, effort is everything.

That particular evening, after Rosemary's phone call, I pulled in the driveway and pushed the button to open the garage door. Torrey was standing in the garage waiting for me with her hands behind her back. I got out of the car and asked her the magic question, already knowing the answer. But she was going to have fun with it. "Torrey, did you remember to bring your spelling book home today?"

"No, Daddy," was Torrey's response, as she tried not to smile. "I forgot."

"What's that behind your back?" I asked.

She turned around trying not to show me her spelling book. Then when I told her to get in the van, she was startled and showed me her book. I told her again to get in the van and indicated that we needed to go for a ride. She asked where we were going, but I didn't tell her. All I said was that we were going to celebrate the fact that she had remembered to bring her spelling book home five days in a row.

Many parents reading this book will have a difficult time wanting to do what we did. It's not what we did, but that we did something fun and out of the ordinary. Celebrating victories by eating food is probably bad for you. Celebrating by eating fat is probably worse. Eating ice cream thirty minutes before dinner time is certainly unforgivable!

We drove straight to an ice cream store, and at that hour, we were the only ones there. I walked in, and when the young man across the counter asked me if he could help us, I responded with "Yes, but first, do you know why we're here?"

He looked a little puzzled and then fearful. He probably wondered what kind of a nut he was alone in the store with! He probably wanted to say, "I hope you're here for ice cream 'cause that's all we have."

When he just looked and didn't say anything, I continued. "We're here because my daughter (pointing at Torrey who was thoroughly embarrassed at this point) did a great job this week. We want the biggest waffle cone you have." I wanted Torrey to hear me brag about her. It wasn't important for me to state the exact triumph, just that we had had one.

Don't do what I did. Celebrate with a tofu burger or a bean sprout cone! But be sure to celebrate the effort and the victory. It's not what a parent does that counts, but that a parent does something.

After that great week of five spelling books in a row, Torrey forgot her spelling book again on Monday. But slowly she got it together. Today she's a rememberer. It didn't happen all at once; she's too smart for that (she takes after her mother). But it did happen. She did learn to accept responsibility without excuse, because she chose to. It was either that or write spelling words until she started receiving her social security checks! Her choice.

SUMMARY

1. Children must be taught that excuses are unacceptable.
2. No-excuse living as an adult takes no-excuse training as a child.
3. Each child in each home is very different. Some are Pleasers and some are Barbarians. The Pleaser will adopt the plan for learning responsibility while the Barbarian will spend time creating excuses.
4. Reward effort.

QUESTIONS

1. In what area of your children's lives do they need help in accepting responsibility?
2. What are the excuses they use to pass the blame?
3. What plan can you use to help him learn no-excuse living?
4. How will you celebrate?

Chapter Seven

————◀◉▶————

First and Last

"What do you look for?" I asked my interviewer. It was my senior year in college, and the corporate headhunters were on campus, conducting interviews with prospective employees. Since I knew I wasn't going to graduate until the next year, I took advantage of the opportunity to go through the interview process for practice. In fact, my major adviser instructed me to interview the interviewers. I mainly wanted to know what they look for in a prospective employee.

"It's probably not what you think," was the answer one interviewer gave me. "Notice I haven't asked you a thing about your transcripts. Grades and course work are the last concern on my list. I'll get to that if and when we get past the first two items on my list. I'm more concerned about what I call your 'first and last.'"

————◀◉▶————

First impressions are all that most people have to go on, and they will open or close many doors.

————◀◉▶————

"First and last." What in the world did he mean by that? He let that phrase sink in before explaining that he was referring to *first* impressions and being able to *last* long enough to finish difficult tasks. Does the prospective employee make a good first impression? Do you want to continue talking to him or her or do you want to end this particular interview as soon as possible? Does the applicant seem to have "the stuff" to be able to stay with a task to its completion?

These are skills that apply to so much more than employability. They are also two of the more significant skills for life. This particular interviewer went on to say that he frequently talks with people who turn him off before they're five minutes into the interview. Their first impression—the way they talk, dress, and handle themselves—is so unappealing that he would be embarrassed for them to represent his company. Many others are so obnoxious or cocky during the interview that he knows he'd be looking for work himself if he recommended them for employment.

"I wish that schools would spend some time teaching kids how to go through an interview," he went on. "In fact, I'd like to teach it. First impressions are all that most people have to go on, and they will open or close many doors."

This interviewer said that there are those who make great first impressions, but that's all they have. He spends enough time talking with each one to get a feeling for whether they finish the things they start. "How could you possibly find that out in an interview?" I remember asking.

"By trying to get them to tell me about some of the meaningful things they've recently done in their lives. One told me that besides his summer job, he and his dad worked at restoring an antique car in the evenings. I asked him if they had finished the car, and he said that they would probably finish it this summer. I learned a lot about him by listening to him talk about working on that long-term project with his dad."

The interviewer said he also tries to find out by discussing different topics if an applicant has many of the qualities that an employer is looking for. Is the applicant a decision maker? How does he or she get along with other people at work? Can the person work alone? How does the person resolve differences of opinion and conflict?

The son in the father-son car team had said that if his father wasn't going to budge on an issue, the son would drop it and move on. "After all, it really is his project I'm working on."

To the interviewer, that showed he was decisive, yet understood authority. He also showed a strong sense of loyalty, another essential character trait. Another quality the interviewer looks for is a "giving nature," an understanding of citizenship, which is just the opposite of the "what am I going to get out of it" mentality that is so common.

FIRST

Though first impressions will probably be one of the last things our children are concerned with, this is an area that parents should decide to teach. Teaching a child to look adults in the eye when they are introduced is part of that first impression. Sticking out a hand and knowing how to shake hands is also part of succeeding at that introduction process. Eye contact, handshake, and then proper verbal responses to the questions an adult might ask—these are positive first-impression makers. It's important to teach a child how to express a genuine interest in the questions that are being asked of him and the statements made to him when he meets people. A fake memorized speech followed by a glazed-over look is not the way to make a good first impression.

> *It's important to teach a child how to express a genuine interest in the questions that are being asked of him and the statements made to him when he meets people.*

"Why do I have to do that?" one child asked her mother. "I don't even want to meet those people who are coming to dinner. Can't I just stay in my room? Can we get a pizza for the kids instead?"

Very few children will want to be a part of these lessons in manners. But proper introductory manners and table manners make positive first impressions. These are the door openers that help give young adults the opportunity to get past the interview and in the door so they can show what they can really do.

One of the easiest ways to prepare a child to be successful at first impressions is to start by acting them out at home. Here's a scenario of what one father did.

"Tommy," his father said, "after dinner we're going to play a game." Tommy's eyes lit up until he heard what the game was. "This Saturday night we are having several people from my office over for dinner. I want you to be the greeter. When they ring the bell, you're to answer the door, introduce yourself, and then invite them in. Tonight we're going to practice doing that. I'm going to go outside, ring the bell, and when you answer the door, I'm going to make believe I'm one of those people who is coming to dinner."

Tommy's dad not only spent that evening teaching his son about introductions, about looking people in the eye and shaking hands, but each time he came in the house he asked Tommy a different question—a question that one of the guests might ask. To make the activity fun, the dad even sprinkled in ridiculous questions such as, "Don't you think your dad is a lot smarter than your mom?" They both laughed as Tommy loosened up and said, "No, my mom is smarter." Dad would march back out of the house.

Then came the night of the dinner party and Tommy was scared to death. Eventually, he began to enjoy his role, as various guests made encouraging comments, such as, "Wow, what a great handshake." Being a greeter was helping to prepare Tommy in that vital area of first impressions.

DECISION MAKER

If you were given the job of creating a new product, the first thing you might ask is "What will this product be expected to do?" That seems to be the same question we should be asking ourselves concerning our children. What will they be required to do or deal with when they come off the production line? Granted, children aren't things coming off an assembly line. But just as the production crew is held responsible for an end result, parents are also responsible to help produce mature adults who have the necessary skills to meet the challenges that are before them.

The interviewer stated that he didn't want a robot. He was looking for people who were decision makers. That's the same ability all parents want for their children. Repeatedly parents ask me, "How do I help my child become a decision maker?" We all want our children to learn how to make decisions for themselves, rather than let others dictate to them or pressure them into doing things they really don't want to do.

The answer has always been the same. If we want our children to be decision makers, if we want them to grow up with the ability to be decisive, if we want them to be leaders rather than peer followers, we need to teach them to make decisions. We teach decision making by giving them decisions to make.

Decision making is a process—and an effort. Some children are born with this ability. They want to make their own decisions, right or wrong. Theirs is not necessarily a decision-making problem as much as it is an authority problem. They're the ones who have a hard time letting anyone teach them to tie their shoes. They have no idea how to tie a bow, but they go ahead to do it anyway. When the parent tries to help, all the child says, repeatedly, is, "Me do it, Mommy!" The scene is one that has a set of big hands being pushed out of the way by a set of pudgy little hands. "No, me do it, Mommy!" This assertion for independence is an initial step in decision making.

Just as the production crew is held responsible for an end result, parents are also responsible to help produce mature adults who have the necessary skills to meet the challenges that are before them.

Many other children would prefer to have their parents make all the decisions for them. Concerned about pleasing or doing it perfectly, they say, "What do you think I should do?" "What do you think I should wear?" "How do you think I should do it?" "Do you think I should go?" Unfortunately, there are many parents who quickly come to the rescue and make the decisions for the child, denying the child the opportunity to learn. But this is not helping or teaching the child to make decisions. This is only postponing the process of learning how to make those decisions.

Eddie's domineering nature didn't help at all when he taught his daughter Rebecca to drive. Every time when she had to pull out onto the highway, she froze. She couldn't decide when it was time to enter

the flow of traffic on the highway. This became a major area of difficulty. Her hesitancy was dangerous. She chose not to drive on any
highway because she just couldn't decide when to pull out.

As Eddie and his wife, Dolores, discussed the problem, it
became apparent that this was a difficulty in many areas of Rebecca's
life. The fear of failure, fear of displeasing her father, and a lack of
practice in decision making had now become very obvious.

In years past, when Rebecca couldn't decide what to wear, her
mother made the decision for her. "If I didn't decide, we would have
been late to church. Becky would have stood in front of that closet
forever," her mother said. When she found it difficult to make other
decisions in her young life, her father made them for her. He thought
he was being helpful. Now, however, he realized that his daughter
was finding it difficult to make most of the important decisions in her
life. The driving incident only made it more evident.

In order for a child to grow up to be an adult who can make
decisions, the task of decision making must be part of the growing-
up process. These are decision opportunities that a parent must provide for the child and then get out of the way, allowing the child to
practice. Use simple decisions at first, then gradually add decisions
that are more difficult. Remember, this is Employability 101.

In the previous chapters, the decision of task completion was
put into the child's path. The child was not forced to take the garbage
out. Instead, the option to take it out or receive the consequence was
offered to the child. The child had to make the decision whether to
continue playing or stop for a moment and take the garbage out. The
decision was the child's.

Parents make far too many decisions for their children. It's a
great decision-making opportunity to leave the young child in a situation where the child has to decide what clothes to wear. Why don't
we do that? A typical parental answer: "He'll take too long to decide
or it will be something totally inappropriate." If we believe that decision making is a necessary skill for adulthood, then we need to adjust
the family curriculum to teach this skill.

For the young child who can't decide what to wear when there
are morning time constraints, create a learning classroom the night

before. "Kelly," the parent could begin, "from now on, you're going to pick out what you will wear to school or to church on the night before. Before you come downstairs for your bedtime snack, you will need to choose the outfit you're going to wear. Put it on the chair by your bed. In the morning it'll be ready for you to wear."

"But you wouldn't believe what outfit my child would choose," you may say.

Then give the child some decision-making parameters. Isn't that the way we live as adults? Isn't that what we do when we buy a car? We go to the car dealer with some limits and guidelines. We need a certain kind of car, and it needs to be in this particular price range. All decisions in life have parameters. Learning how to make decisions within those parameters is very important.

To set those parameters with your child, try saying something like this: "This evening after dinner you and I are going to rearrange your closet. On one side we're going to put the clothes that you can wear to school. In the middle will be your special clothes, things for parties and for church. On the other side we're going to hang your play clothes. Each night before school you can select clothes from the school side, not an outfit from the play-clothes side.

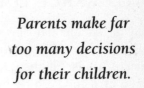

Parents make far too many decisions for their children.

Some children will persist in choosing an outfit that is unacceptable, that doesn't fit the parameters. Then roll out the consequence. The Barbarian will quite naturally choose to wear inappropriate items. Here's an example of what a parent might say to a child: "When you have selected what you want to wear tomorrow and come down for your before-bed snack, if you choose again from the wrong group of clothes like you did yesterday, there will be no snack. Choose from the section that is for school, not from the section that is for play."

Give the child the job of choosing. If she chooses from the wrong section and you're sure it's a rebellion issue, invoke the consequence. If she really didn't understand, clearly state the parameters. Then get out of the way and once again put her into the mode of choosing.

Decision making can be practiced in many areas of a child's life. Few decisions are more significant than those involving the handling of money. (Chapter 13 is devoted to that important lesson.) One example of decision making that utilizes money pertains to the young child and the grocery store. Many times moms feel like they are held hostage when they push their shopping cart toward the exit of the grocery store. There at the exit, the mom is ambushed by small vending machines that offer globs, plastic helmets, plastic rings, rubber insects, and gum. Leaving the store becomes a contest of wills. Children, after being told repeatedly in the store that they can't have the junk-food cereal or the in-vogue cookies they see on television, spy one last opportunity for junk. They now beg loudly or adhere themselves to the pole that holds up the glass sphere displaying the "treasures" that are only twenty-five cents. Under these conditions, it is Mom who is forced into decision-making mode. Should she give in and buy this junk for the child, or should she stand her ground and struggle to get past the ambush? If only there was a back door!

ALLOWANCE TIME

Giving children an allowance can be a great opportunity for them. The decision of whether or not to buy a "glob" should be put into the child's hands. Children should be given an allowance at a young age. At four, a child can be given an allowance of ten dimes. The dimes will be found lying around the house until the child learns that these pieces of metal can be exchanged for globs and helmets.

"Danny," Mom can begin, "we're going to the grocery store this morning. Go get your G. I. Joe wallet, because you might want to buy something with your allowance. You might want to buy one of the helmets you've asked for before. I'm not going to buy them for you anymore because you have your own money now. That's one of the things you can use your money for."

Deciding what to spend your money on is a very important decision-making process. The young child at first will quite naturally spend everything on globs or helmets. Later, baseball cards may be the attraction, with the justification that it's an investment! These are decision-making skills that every adult will need. Eventually the child will learn to resist these globs in order to save up for something more important, like a giant, battery-powered water gun!

A HEALTHY UNDERSTANDING OF AUTHORITY

Two new counselors came to work at Sheridan House the same summer. Both had just graduated from college. They were the same age, yet they had very different attitudes about the concept of authority. John did nothing but say, "Yes, sir." He never questioned anything we did or asked, he just said, "Yes, sir," and obediently did what he was told.

Lenny, on the other hand, questioned everything. Every time we discussed something with him or asked him to do something, he questioned our decisions and experience. It became exhausting to work with him.

Staff meetings became interesting with these two on board. Lenny made every discussion a debate. In reality, he made a habit of questioning authority. John, on the other hand, was worthless in a staff meeting. He never had an opinion. Or if he did, he never expressed it. He had been taught to put his brain in park and never question those in authority. Nice thought for his superiors, but that meant his brain was absent from our "brain trust" when we got together to make decisions. We might as well not invite him to the staff meetings and just send him a memo with our final decision.

Lenny caused conflicts at staff meetings. John just took up a chair. One made an art of questioning authority, while the other offered no opinion around any authority. When the summer was done, unbeknownst to them, we had to choose one of these summer workers to continue with us on a full-time basis. As the senior staff met to discuss this dilemma, we realized that we wanted a combination of each young man. We wanted someone who had an opinion, was able to express it, and then was able to move on past that opinion to get the job done, whether we did it his way or not. A senior staff member defined our need when she said, "I don't particularly like the word *assertive*, but I do believe it applies here. I think we're looking for people to join the team and be 'respectfully assertive' with their opinions."

RESPECTFULLY ASSERTIVE

Children need to be able to question opinions and directions. That's often the only way they will ever come to understand the "whys" and the "whats" about the directions of those in authority. This very valuable skill for employees helps an organization grow. The difficulty arises in knowing when to question the decisions of those in authority and just how to go about doing it.

Why?

It is very important for children to learn that it is okay to respectfully question those in authority, because there might be a time when those in authority ask them to do something that is morally wrong. Children need to be able to discern when and when not to question authority.

How?

Learning how to question authority starts with the way parents handle a child during a confrontation. The child should be treated and spoken to in a respectful way. That teaches the child to respond to the parent respectfully. Here's an example of how a parent should respond to a child who has just protested with a noisy, disrespectful outburst when he's been told he will be sent to bed early: "Billy, you need to calm down and talk to me in a respectful way or, not only will this discussion be over, you will be sent to bed immediately, rather than at eight." The parent talks firmly, yet calmly, looking Billy right in the eye. If Billy doesn't calm down, he's going to bed. If Billy does calm down, the parent can say, "Now that's better. Let's sit down and discuss why you think I'm wrong to send you to bed early."

Sound impossible? It's difficult, but not impossible. For the parent to respond to Billy's outburst with a parental outburst only teaches Billy that it's proper to disagree by yelling.

Parents should encourage their children to express their opinions. Everyone has an opinion. The key is to help children learn to disagree in an agreeable manner. The greatest amount of work will be on the part of the parent. Once again, this is a job that takes extra time.

It's much more expedient to act like a drill sergeant and say, "Do it!" in a very authoritarian manner. That might get the job done quickly, but it also teaches the child some very negative habits. Children with a drill sergeant for a parent find their own ways to rebel since they aren't allowed to give their own opinions. This also teaches them that when they are older, they will be able to impose their ways in an authoritarian manner on those under them—a spouse, children, employees. Unfortunately, the lesson many other children learn is that the opinions they have must be worthless, since the most important people in their lives don't want to hear their opinions.

When?

Learning when to question authority is equally significant. When Robey was in elementary school, he had a soccer coach who had obviously not been around children much. During the preseason practices, I would arrive early to pick Robey up and be shocked at this coach's language. He'd stand in the middle of the field, with a half-eaten cigar hanging out of his mouth, screaming at the boys to work harder. Every now and then there would be a four-letter word sprinkled in.

He'd obviously watched the movie *Patton* too many times! As preseason continued, I noticed more and more parents arriving to "observe" practice. Word about his coaching approach had gotten around. As I stood on the sidelines one day watching practice, two moms walked up to me and said, "We've talked to the soccer league commissioner and they're not going to do anything about the way the coach talks to the boys. We've both decided that today's the last day our boys are going to be on this team. What are you going to do?"

Employable individuals are those who understand respect for those in authority and yet are able to respect their own opinions enough to express them properly.

My answer, I realized, could be very incriminating. If I left Robey on the team, was I a poor parent, not protecting him from this poor role model? I told them I hadn't decided.

The next day, walking out of a staff meeting at Sheridan House, Steve, one of the ex-college athletes on staff, asked me about Robey. "How's soccer going?" It was just an innocent question to show his interest in my children, but it opened the door for me to say, "Funny that you should ask. I'm thinking about pulling him out. He has a horrible coach." I went on to describe some of the difficulties we were having.

Steve responded with a twinkle in his eye. "Sounds like he's getting good practice for some of the bad coaches and teachers and grumpy bosses he's going to have in the future! We all need that kind of practice."

Part of what Steve said was a joke. But he was right. This could be good practice. Robey stayed on that team that season. I hung around a lot more than I had done in previous years and every day after practice we discussed what went on. We discussed why the coach yelled at the boys so much, why he used the language he did, and how Robey could best approach him. Together we decided that it would be good for Robey to pick a time to ask the coach if he could talk to him for a minute privately. We even rehearsed out loud what Robey would say, with me yelling back at him. We also talked about earning the right to question people in authority by working hard at practice.

Robey did talk with his coach one day after practice. He asked him all the right questions. It didn't change the way the coach talked to or treated the boys. In fact, it barely changed the way the coach treated Robey. But it did give Robey some practice that was far more significant than soccer practice. It gave him an opportunity to practice respectful assertiveness. It gave him an opportunity to practice respect for authority while not being afraid to ask questions.

If Richard Nixon had had men around him who respectfully questioned the decisions he was making concerning the cover-up of Watergate, he might have been able to finish out his term as president. Instead, they just followed blindly and said, "Yes, sir," and they all failed together. Employable individuals are those who understand respect for those in authority and yet are able to respect their own opinions enough to express them properly. That skill might just keep some kids from following cult leaders or gang members. It will certainly make them valuable employees and team players.

SUMMARY

1. An employable person is someone who is raised with a good "First and Last." They make a good first impression and are able to last all the way through to the end of the project.
2. An employable person needs to be able to make decisions.
3. A good employee and coworker understands respectful assertiveness
4. It's the parents' job to prepare a child by teaching the "Firsts and Lasts."

QUESTIONS

1. Take a look at your parenting style. Do you allow your child to ask questions about decisions that you make?
2. Do you make all the decisions for your child?
3. What decisions could you begin turning over to your child? What parameters do you need to set?
4. What learning situations could you put in your child's "curriculum" that would help your child develop skills in "Firsts and Lasts"?

Chapter Eight

Could Your Child Answer the Call?

Several years ago a wealthy friend called me with exciting news. "I don't know if you've heard," he began, "but we've broken up our estate and given my son Jonathan his share of the estate now, while we're still alive. His share amounts to almost a hundred million dollars. I want you to fly out here and talk to him about the children's homes at Sheridan House. He's in a position to be able to help you buy that land you've been looking at."

Jonathan was this man's thirty-eight-year-old son—a nice guy, who knew that his father was a longtime supporter of Sheridan House, as well as hundreds of other charities. With all this newfound wealth now under his own control for the first time, this would be Jonathan's first opportunity to get involved in giving. I immediately called Jonathan's office, set an appointment, and got a plane ticket.

The lunch with Jonathan was very interesting. We spent much of the lunch talking about what this money would mean to him. In the month since he had begun receiving his money, he had already purchased a condo at a ski resort in Utah, and he was looking at a ranch in Wyoming. He was also in the process of having a boat built that would be docked by the family's home in Florida. He was still a nice guy, but a nice guy on a buying frenzy. Preparing for this new wealth had caused Jonathan to spend time planning for all the things he was going to get. Doing anything benevolent with this money had never entered his mind. Not because he was greedy, he had simply never thought about giving anything to anyone other than himself.

At the end of the luncheon Jonathan handed me a check for Sheridan House for a thousand dollars. We said good-bye and I caught a plane back to south Florida. Later that month I got a phone call from Jonathan's father. He wanted to know what his son had done for Sheridan House.

"I heard that you met with Jonathan. He told me that he gave you a check for Sheridan House." I confirmed that Jonathan had given us a donation and that we were very grateful. The father continued, "To tell you the truth, I was greatly relieved to hear that he did that. The other charities that we support said he had decided not to give them anything. 'Maybe next year,' was his response to their requests." After a few seconds of silence he finally asked the question he really wanted to ask. "Bob, do you mind if I ask how much Jonathan gave to Sheridan House?" This was the question I was dreading. "Mr. Jones," I began, "Jonathan graciously gave us a gift of one thousand dollars." I knew this was not the amount that this father had in mind. Not after giving his son close to one hundred million dollars. After several seconds of silence this distraught father said, as much to himself as to me, "It's my fault. I spent a lifetime teaching him how to get. I never taught him how to give."

This father realized too late that he had sent his son out the door without any understanding of the responsibility we all have to give some of our resources to those in need. This is an area of citizenship that requires us to do something for the betterment of others, even though it yields nothing materially for us personally.

John F. Kennedy gave us Camelot's golden rule when he said in his 1961 inaugural address, "Ask not what your country can do for you, but what you can do for your country." To the contrary, at least two generations of adults have held the parenting philosophy, "I want

> *Children have grown up learning only how to get. When they have become adults, they quite naturally continued under the premise that they are here to get.*

my children to have the things I never had." Children have grown up learning only how to get. When they have become adults, they quite naturally continued under the premise that they are here to get. The mature attitude of giving instead of always getting doesn't automatically come with the onset of puberty. It must be taught.

TEACHING RESPONSIBILITY TOWARD OTHERS

Teaching the concept of reaching beyond your own needs to help meet needs of others is a lesson that must be begun at an early age. It is directly opposite of the lessons taught in today's culture. Our society teaches us to ask ourselves, "Why would I give, when I get nothing in return?" We are blasted with slogans such as: *Have it your way! You asked for it, you got it! You deserve a break today!* Our society markets a way of thinking that says, "Take care of number one only."

Each year at Sheridan House we have many church groups come to our campuses on Saturdays and volunteer to paint the outside of our buildings. I usually go and talk to them before they begin the project. Years ago a man stood up and asked a question about the upcoming weekend's paint project: "Do you mind if I bring my son?" There was grumbling in the ranks as he asked that question. One man went so far as to say, "We don't want to be there all day. We could get this painting done in four or five hours if we get right down to it. This is not a shop class. Let's not get bogged down with baby-sitting."

Immediately the pastor of this group responded: "You know I think that's a great idea. If we change our plans a little to help teach our kids, not so much to paint, but more about their responsibility to help others, we'll be teaching them a lot. That way, thirty years from now there will be men here to help Sheridan House in the next generation."

Years ago there were many more opportunities to help others. When a barn burned down the whole community arrived on the scene and began rebuilding. They didn't give of their very precious time because they were getting anything back. They helped each other because they understood it as part of their civic responsibility.

NO MORE BARNS

There aren't any more barns burning down in my neighborhood, but the principle remains true. In fact, the concept of going the extra mile caused Sheridan House to pick the particular golf course we picked for our annual golf tournament. For years we had played at one particular country club. The club employees had neatly divided up their areas of responsibility—so neatly that, when we piled into the country club with three hundred players and got bottlenecked at the check-in counter, no one left their assigned post even for a moment to help the harried guys behind the counter get the golf bags out of the cars and on to the golf carts. It wasn't part of their job. They stood and watched the logjam of cars and players.

This concept of learning to be observant of the needs around you is not easy to teach, especially when we are so interested in communicating our needs to those around us.

The next year we decided to try a new country club for our tournament. That day when the golfers started arriving, I anticipated the same logjam and delay. Not this time. Every employee from lawn maintenance to the pro came to the golf-club drop area the minute they saw that their coworkers needed help. No one even needed to page them. It was natural for them to cross over the line of their job description to please the client and get the job done. They were more interested in the needs of the team than their own. We've never gone back to the other country club.

THE TEAM CONCEPT

"I didn't leave that there!" "That's not mine!" "That's Billy's job!" Those are all the anti-team statements that children quite naturally learn to use when they are asked to do something they don't want to do. It often works because their statement is true. It might not be their particular area of responsibility, but neither was that burned-down barn.

We need to acknowledge that they're correct: The items they are being asked to bring into the house are not theirs. Then we need to make a statement such as "They are shoes that belong to this family, however. Pick them up and put them in Billy's room please."

To ask why I have to do something that's not my job is a legitimate question. It needs to be answered. A child needs to do a particular job because he belongs to the family team. Though the child's first team is his family, as an adult he will be part of many other, larger teams such as his marriage, his church, his place of employment, and especially forgotten in this time in history, his nation.

After hearing this particular talk at a seminar, Luke and his wife, Jana, came up to the book table to say, "The need to work together as a team became very evident to us recently through a statement made by our twelve-year-old son, Jerry." Luke relayed the story.

"Jerry was sitting in the kitchen talking to his mother. She was listening, while frantically running around the kitchen trying to get the table set and dinner ready. Walking in from work, I noticed how overwhelmed she was and that Jerry was just sitting there, so I said, 'Jerry why don't you help your mom instead of just sitting there?'

"Jana replied, 'Oh, that's okay, he's keeping me company.' Then Jerry said quite innocently, 'Yeah, this is her job. I've been working in school all day.'" This couple stopped in the middle of the kitchen and just looked at each other. What were they teaching him? Were they teaching him when someone needs help, don't offer any unless asked? And then decide if you really want to step over the job description boundaries and help?

It was important for this couple to reevaluate what it was they were teaching. Were they raising a child who would be conscious of the needs of those around him? Or would he just look out for his own needs and wants?

This concept of learning to be observant of the needs around you is not easy to teach, especially when we are so interested in communicating *our* needs to those around us. Our radar dishes are turned around. We've been taught to broadcast our needs rather than receive information on the needs of others.

EXAMPLE

Teaching this concept starts with being an example. It's hard to teach children the concept of meeting needs when one parent is watching television or reading the paper while the other is struggling to get dinner on or homework done. We can't expect the children to learn what we're not willing to model. One of the biggest motivators for those country club employees at our golf tournament had to be the fact that the club pro himself was setting the example by helping to move the golf bags.

We can't expect the children to learn what we're not willing to model.

Time at home just after work offers one of the best opportunities of the day for relaxation. A time to take a break and sit with no responsibility. It also offers one of the most teachable moments of the day. "What can I do to help?" is the magic teaching phrase. This offer does more than just help with the hassles of the moment that the other spouse might be dealing with. It also helps set the child on the right path for the future.

SET THE PLAN IN PLACE

"Jerry," his dad began, "from now on when one of us comes through the kitchen and sees that Mom needs help, it will be our job to stop what we're doing and lend a hand. I have an even better idea. When we see Mom doing something, it will be our job to ask what we can do to help. 'What can I do to help, Mom?' will be the question to ask."

Then Jana, Jerry's mom, piped in with, "It's not just the question, but the way you respond when I admit that I do need help. A sour face makes the offer worthless. It lets me know that even though you're asking me, Jerry, you don't really care to help me."

A pained expression or a sigh of resignation is a natural response from a child. Why should we expect them to automatically want to do something extra? It's our job, however, to teach the attitude as well as the task.

"Jerry, if you fail to ask or if you ask and then have a bad attitude when Mom tells you that she does have something for you to do, you'll be washing the dishes by yourself that night."

"But Dad, what if I forget?" Jerry protested. "I wasn't sitting and watching her work on purpose. I just didn't think about it."

"That's just the point," Luke responded. "Up until now, Mom hasn't asked you to help for two reasons. First was because she didn't have time to deal with a 'lemon face' when she asked for help. It was just less draining for her to do it herself. The second reason was because she enjoys your company and she didn't want to scare you off. She knows that you *do* work hard all day. But so does she. We want to help you learn to notice when people around you need help.

"It all hit me the other day," Luke told his son, "when I saw one of the guys at work going back and forth in front of my office door with boxes of files. I got up and asked him what he was doing. He told me he was bringing in boxes from the back of his station wagon. I asked if I could help and he said, 'That would be great!' Together we made a dozen trips, carrying boxes of files. When it was all done I went back into my office. A while later he came back down to my office. 'Thanks for helping me with those boxes. I'd still be there if it weren't for you.' Then I said that I was surprised that no one else offered when I had asked him if he needed help, since we were standing in front of four or five other guys. 'In fact,' I said, 'I expected them to follow us out to your car.'

"You know what he said to me, Jerry?" this dad concluded. "He said, 'A man could have a heart attack in front of these guys and they'd step over him. The atmosphere is so self-centered here. You're the one everyone can always count on to help. Thanks!'"

"Mr. Robinson said that?" Jana said incredulously.

"Yes, he did. He was visibly moved that I would help him for no apparent gain." Smiling, Luke said, "I'm glad *my* dad taught me to ask my mom if she needed help."

BUT WE'RE MAKING HIM

One woman asked the question, "What good is it if we *make* our children do it? They're not really volunteering. We're making them ask us if we need help."

Few children will find it natural to volunteer to do extra work. Most children must first be taught to be aware of the needs of others. Then, in time, they will more naturally step in to help. Children have to be taught to take a bath. They wouldn't understand the need on their own until they became adults and people were repulsed by their odor. After a period of being taught, they understand the need, and they bathe without being told. The same concept is true for volunteering. Rather than wait until they're adults and their self-centered attitudes repulse the people around them, parents would do better to prepare them early.

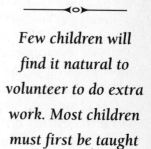

Few children will find it natural to volunteer to do extra work. Most children must first be taught to be aware of the needs of others.

MAKE HIM A RECIPIENT AS WELL

You never seem to see the value of the team concept so well as when it's *your* barn that is being rebuilt. Then you become grateful for the volunteer attitude around you. Luke remembered that very day. It was Saturday morning and Jerry was out front grumbling through one of his chores. He had to wash his mom's car every Saturday. One Saturday while he was washing the car, Luke came out, grabbed a rag and started helping his son. "What are you doing?" Jerry asked his dad, staring in disbelief. "Why are you helping me?"

"I had some extra time," this father explained. "Since I've finished my chores, I thought I'd come out and help you get this car done."

Prior to this, Jerry was never conscious of the fact that his parents helped him do anything. In fact, this boy thought he existed solely to help them get their work done. That his father stepped out and helped for no apparent reason other than he wanted to help his son was a big statement. It helped to drive home the concept of going the extra mile. A son got to experience it firsthand. He was now on the receiving end.

Would this lesson help to make him a good citizen or employee? Not long ago a popular Miami Dolphins linebacker, John Offerdahl, was speaking to his employees just before the opening of one of his new bagel shops (Offerdahl's Gourmet Bagels). The new shop was in a shopping center that was across the street and about a hundred yards from one of south Florida's ever-present roadside canals.

As John was in his store making a presentation to his employees, he heard a loud screeching of tires and turned around just in time to see a car go careening off the road into the canal. Automatically, John ran out of the store, across the parking lot, and arrived just as the car was going under water. He dove into the water and rescued the elderly couple. As he pulled them on shore, the police and rescue squad arrived to take over. After being assured that the couple was going to be all right, John walked back across the street and continued his meeting.

His employees were in shock and asked, "Why did you do that?"

"Just an automatic response, I guess," John answered. "I didn't mean to be heroic or anything." In fact, John was rather embarrassed about the whole event. Later on when the publicity got out, John didn't want to even talk to the reporters. "I'm no hero," he said later. "I just did what anybody else would do. I happened to be the one who was there to see the need."

Unfortunately, John was wrong when he made that statement. The fact that his actions gained so much publicity showed that his response is no longer the natural thing for a citizen to do. We are no longer barn builders or canal divers in this culture. That's more of an extra mile than we've been taught to walk. John exemplified an attitude that it was only natural to help those around you who are in need. That's just the kind of attitude we need to teach our children. Will it impact their employment and citizenship skills? One of John's employees commented some time later, "It occurred to several of us who work for Offerdahl Bagels, that if he would risk his life like that for perfect strangers, he would certainly be a person that employees could count on if they needed help. It's nice to work for someone who's not self-centered."

SUMMARY

1. Children must be taught the concept of seeing when people around them are in need of help.
2. That concept of citizenship starts in the home.
3. Citizenship doesn't come naturally. Children must be required to learn that if any family member needs a hand it's their responsibility to help out.
4. Teaching a child the team concept will impact his marriage, his employability, and his response to his nation. If they need him he'll be able to respond.

QUESTIONS

1. What areas come to mind when you think about one family member standing around watching another family member work?
2. How could the children be taught to help their fellow family members?
3. What is the explanation and plan you will use when you talk to the children about this process?
4. What can you do to make the children become recipients of this "barn building"?

PART 3

———◦———

Raising a Marriageable Child

Chapter Nine

------◄◦►------

Preparing for a Partner

Bonnie and her father had just finished the arduous task trying to make the best selection. After weeks of reading and then comparing what they read to the actual physical appearance, they were now able to decide which one was best for her. Looks weren't on the top of her list, but they were important to her. He father, on the other hand, was more concerned with reliability and finances. He wanted to make sure that his daughter's final choice took good care of her after she left home.

It's amazing how much time this father and daughter spent discussing and researching the purchase of her first car. They had implemented the same decision-making process they used when she was selecting a college. Without utilizing some sort of preestablished decision-making strategy, however, Bonnie would have been a sitting duck when she arrived at the auto dealership. Many of the more important decisions she had to make needed to have been thought through before she was actually making the selection.

College selection and the purchase of a first car are very important decisions. Without the benefit of outside help, individuals can make decisions based on emotions alone. As important as selecting the right college or purchasing a good, affordable car is, it is far less significant than selecting the right spouse. Why is it that we leave our children without any skills in spouse selection? Their selection of a spouse is usually left to emotional responses. And the exorbitant price of making a subjective decision like that will be paid out over a lifetime.

MAKING THE SELECTION

One of the most important skills we need to teach our children is how to think through the selection of a spouse. It's too late to be discussing that process if we wait until our children are twenty-two years old and very involved with a potential marriage partner. These discussions must take place even before the dating process begins, and then they need to continue, from time to time, up until a marriage actually takes place.

"What do you believe are important things to look for in a date or especially in a husband?" Eric asked his fifteen-year-old, Ashley.

"What do you mean, Daddy?" Ashley responded.

> *The discussions of the attributes of a spouse need to take place long before a young person is emotionally entrenched in a relationship.*

This father and daughter were sitting in a restaurant for their monthly meal out together. This was a long-standing father/daughter tradition. Generally, Eric let his children each discuss whatever they wanted to when he took them out alone on dates. But this was the evening, as difficult as it was for him, that he decided to begin the process teaching his daughter how to think about important character traits of a husband.

"If you were to describe the perfect husband for yourself, what would be important to you?" Eric asked Ashley again.

After a few moments of awkwardness, this question opened up a discussion that lasted an hour and a half. The biggest thing Eric needed to do was restrain himself. He had to realize that his daughter was only fifteen years old. The important attributes that Ashley was stating now, were not necessarily the attributes that she would hold at the top of her list over the next eight years. And this was her list, not his. He knew that he needed to allow it to be hers.

There was one undeniable attribute that was to maintain the top position on Ashley's list over the next eight years. She knew that her husband would need to be in one accord with her Christian faith. The second place spot, however, went from "enjoying the same kind of music" at fifteen years old, to making sure he was "selecting a career that would make money" on her list when she was seventeen. When she was eighteen, the second place had changed to "making sure he agreed with her about not having children." She had just finished a summer of baby-sitting for some very undisciplined preschoolers.

The key in this process was the initial establishment of some basic attributes on a list. They were written that night on a napkin in the restaurant. Eric then asked Ashley to date the list and transfer it to her journal. Several months later Ashley's mother sat on the side of her bed and asked if she could see the list. Ashley then reviewed it and made some modifications. Some priorities had changed in Ashley's life in the past few months.

This process of reviewing Ashley's list every few months, continued all through high school. When Ashley returned home from her first year of college, at the beginning of her summer break, she went out to eat with her dad and he asked her to bring her journal. Knowing what he was wanting to talk about prompted Ashley to say, "You know, I was looking at my Partner List one night this past semester, Dad. I opened to it by accident, and as I looked at it, I wondered if I'm ever going to find the guy on my list. He doesn't seem to go to the same college I go to." Eric knew that this was a time to deal with her discouragement more than her list.

The first thing this dad did was analyze the list with her to see if it was unrealistic. After making a minor alteration they decided that it was still the proper list to use for helping to make a decision. Then Eric talked to his daughter about making the decision not to settle for second best. That was an easy discussion, since Ashley wasn't involved with anyone at that moment.

In her junior year of college Ashley fell in love. Over spring break she brought the new boyfriend home to meet her family. Both Eric and his wife were actually startled at how good-looking this college athlete was. He seemed like a nice boy, but by the end of one week of talking with him at the house, both parents had some concerns. They decided to keep their thoughts to themselves until Ashley came home again in May.

The minute their daughter walked in the door for her summer vacation, both parents could tell she had something on her mind. Sitting down in the living room, Ashley made the announcement. "Dad," Ashley began, "Troy wants to get engaged over the Fourth of July weekend." There was a long pause. And then Ashley continued, "I really don't know what to do. I love being with him. He's lots of fun and we have a great time. I think I love him. But I keep having these hesitations. Is that natural? I just don't know what to do."

After another moment of silence in the living room, Eric finally said, "Why don't we put on a pot of coffee while you unpack your journal. I'd like to pray about this discussion and then run Troy by your Partner List."

Ashley defensively fired back with "Nobody's going to meet all those things on that stupid list." This time the discussion wasn't going to be quite so easy. It was going to be Ashley's list versus Ashley's emotions. The key here was that it was *Ashley's* list.

"Maybe not, honey," Eric continued while trying to keep his composure, "but it seems like a good place to start. You asked us how to decide about Troy. I think you started making that kind of decision several years ago. Lets see if he's close to the same guy you've been describing."

That weekend was very emotional for a daughter and her parents. Ashley opened up her journal and started reading the first few attributes. Instantly it became apparent that Troy was not even close to the young man she had been describing all these years. Without saying a word, Ashley's parents watched her continue to read the list. All of a sudden she looked down at the floor and said with tears flooding down her face, "He's not the one, is he? I'm settling for a handsome face, aren't I?" Her parents concurred and as they moved over next to her on the couch, they sat and cried together. Together they helped Ashley plot out her next move concerning Troy.

LEFT WITHOUT A YARDSTICK

If we don't teach our child about the selection process, they will be left only with the cultural process of looks and lust. He will select with his eyes and she will select with her expectations of what she thinks he will be like. He makes his selection by looking at her and letting his biology kick in. She, on the other hand, makes her decision after spending a period of time dating him, thinking that his behavior would be the same after they got married. Neither of them realize that dating is the great cultural lie! She'll never again look as lovely as she does while they are dating. He'll never again act (and "act" is an appropriate word here) as good as he does when they are dating.

This whole dating process is a great deception. And we parents leave our children to make life's greatest relationship decision based solely on this deception. We might as well just drop our children off at the used car lot with money sticking out of their pockets, and tell them to find a way home!

The discussions of the attributes of a spouse need to take place long before a young person is emotionally entrenched in a relationship. Once a young person believes that he or she is in love, it's too late for a parent to start asking questions like "What do you think are important attributes of a spouse?" The young person's heart will guide him toward describing the person he's involved with. He will filter his list through his potential spouse, rather than filter his potential spouse through a long-standing list.

THE LIST

A list that is written and repeatedly discussed over a period of years will provide a great decision-making tool for parent and young

> *This whole dating process is a great deception. And we parents leave our children to make life's greatest relationship decision based solely on this deception. We might as well just drop our children off at the used car lot with money sticking out of their pockets, and tell them to find a way home!*

person. A list that the young person feels is truly his or hers, rather than something that a parent has imposed. A list that can be used later and seen as an objective analysis of potential spouses. That's why it's important to take the time to allow the young person the opportunity to hone his or her own list. A list that's imposed is a list that will be ignored when a difficult decision needs to be made.

---◄○►---

Without a selection tool, people will make decisions about spouses using their eyes, biology, or emotions rather than their wisdom.

---◄○►---

When it boils down to a decision of the heart versus the long-standing Partner List, the young person could easily abandon a list that has been forced upon her, by saying, "That's not my list anyway, it's yours."

Ashley had been given the freedom and time to develop her own list with input and guidance from her parents. But it was still her list. There were many times when her father had to bite his tongue as Ashley put various attributes on the list that he knew were not as important as others that were left off. There was even one occasion when Ashley used the list to express frustration with her dad. He knew Ashley was mad at him for a decision he had made. At breakfast one morning out, she altered her list to reflect her anger. She said that the number two thing she wanted to make sure of was that she married a man who was not rigid and stubborn. He knew what she was talking about, but he didn't bite the lure and get into an argument. Giving Ashley the freedom to develop the list was very important. Eventually freedom led to responsibility. She started honing her list to reflect very significant attributes rather than statements of rebellion.

When it came time to look at the list, it was apparent to Ashley that she would be letting herself down if she settled for Troy. Even though her parents had helped her create her list, it was still *her* list. How could she betray herself? As hard as the decision was to break up with Troy, her long-standing, constantly improving list stared her right in the face. The same list that she used to laugh at with her parents and say, "This is stupid; why do we have to do this?" was the list that saved her.

Ashley was prepared to enter into the partner selection process using more than her eyes and her emotions. She had a plan, a constant reminder that this was a very important decision, one that could not be made on the basis of emotions or biology. Instead, this decision needed to be handled with great thought and prayer. Never settling for something that was obviously far below the standard of the list. Never thinking for a moment that "it would be okay

> *A parent might never know exactly how much a child is learning. It's important to teach the important lessons whether or not the young person seems to grasp the magnitude.*

if he wasn't what I have on my list. I'll marry him and then change him." Ashley had a seven-year history of developing a list that helped her make the difficult decision of waiting for the right person rather than settling.

WORTH THE EFFORT

Eric had to constantly remind himself that this was worth the effort even when his daughter was younger and would say the list was stupid or that she didn't want to do it. Especially when his often immature daughter would put things on the list that he felt were irrelevant to a good marriage.

Eric hung in because he had the advantage of hearing another father talk about how his time of discussing a list with his son had saved the young man from a catastrophe. Slowly Ashley began to understand the magnitude of the issue by the way it was revisited a few times a year. The amount of time her parents put into discussing this list added validity to it.

The biggest stamp of importance came when Eric had a business trip to the city where Ashley was in college. He called Ashley ahead of time to set up a dinner. When he called he said, "How 'bout bringing your journal?" Ashley later recounted that that statement helped her realize that her dad was even thinking about her selection process when she was a thousand miles away. She never forgot that.

Whether or not Ashley caught the importance of this list was not the key issue. A parent might never know exactly how much a child is learning. It's important to teach the important lessons whether or not the young person seems to grasp the magnitude. Better to get ten years down the road and be able to say, "I'm glad I did," rather than have to say, "I wish I had."

WHAT HAPPENED TO ASHLEY?

Ashley didn't settle for the wrong person. But she did have to settle for a wait of two more years. All the time, she was thinking that once she left the college campus without a potential marriage partner she was doomed to be an "old maid." Two years later, well after graduation, Ashley went on to meet another young man and they eventually got married. He had the most important qualifications on the list. As of the writing of this book, they are serving in a very dynamic ministry together. None of this would have happened if Ashley had not been prepared to make the tough decision of selecting the right spouse for herself. It took years of training, but in so doing, she avoided years of pain.

SUMMARY

1. Part of the preparation for marriage is to have a tool for selecting whom to marry.
2. Without a selection tool, people will make decisions about spouses using their eyes, biology, or emotions rather than their wisdom.
3. A Partner List helps a young person begin thinking about the important attributes of a spouse long before they are in the position of having to make those decisions and long before the emotions become overwhelming.

4. The Partner List needs to be revisited several times a year so the young person has the privilege of making changes in the attributes on the list.

5. A young person needs to have the freedom to work on and hone the list himself or herself.

QUESTIONS

1. Set a time to take a child out and discuss the attributes of a spouse.

2. Let the young person create his own list. Notice that there have been no suggestions other than a shared commitment to Christ be number one on the list. Parents need to guide the development of this list but not mandate it.

3. Set times to revisit this list regularly. Make sure that you allow the young person to feel as if this is his or her list.

4. When the young person is dating, feel free to call on the list to help your child look at the direction he or she is taking. Does her dating life match her marital list? Remind him (though he will get tired of hearing it) that people do tend to marry a person that they date.

Chapter Ten

◄○►

Practice Makes Prepared

Nick was sitting in front of me at lunch, bemoaning his daughter Pam's dating behavior. It all came to a head due to an incident that took place at his house the previous Friday night. "Pam just started dating a few months ago, and it's making me crazy. She's a great kid and does everything we ask her to, but this dating thing just isn't going the way it should be. I mean there's something wrong." Nick rattled on and on, finally getting to the incident that was the red flag. "She's waited so long to be able to have a boyfriend. I hate to interfere but ... well, last Friday night, right in the living room, in front of all of us, she was sitting on his lap, and then she kissed him on the cheek. Right there in front of us," he repeated, raising his voice.

"I don't want to sound like an overprotective father. Nor do I want to sound like a father who is jealous of his daughter's affections. But something seems inappropriate here! At the very least, we were all very uncomfortable."

"Nick," I asked when he finally settled down, "You're a hunter, have you ever let your son Mica use a gun?"

Nick looked at me, trying to find the connection between his daughter's dating and his son's shooting. Then he answered a little hesitantly, "Yes, as a matter of fact, I bought him a shotgun for his seventeenth birthday. Why?"

"Well, did you just hand him the gun and say, 'Here it is son, take it outside and have a great time. See you when you come home'?"

"Heavens, no!" Nick blurted out. "That would be crazy. A gun is a great responsibility. It can either hurt you, or it can be an instrument of a lot of fun. I did the same thing my father did with me."

"What was that?" I asked, drawing Nick further into the process.

"The first thing my dad did was set an age that I would be allowed to use his shotgun. I remember that I couldn't wait. Then when I reached that magic age, he took me into the garage and put his shotgun out on the workbench. I got to hold his gun and we took it apart and cleaned it together. While we were working on his gun, he was talking to me about safety. We spent that morning talking about the do's and don'ts of using a shotgun. I thought he would never finish. Then finally he took me out to a field and I got to shoot his gun. I can remember that like it was yesterday."

While Nick was staring off into nostalgia, I asked two more questions. "How long before you got to use a gun by yourself?"

"Oh, it was a long time before he would let me go off into the field alone with his gun," was the response.

"When did you get your own gun?"

"I always knew that he was going to buy me a gun for my seventeenth birthday. It was part of the plan. I knew

You wouldn't just hand a child a gun and say, 'Have fun.' Why are you doing that with dating?

that if I showed I could be mature with the way I handled his gun, he'd get me one of my own. It was a big day, but it was also a day I worked hard for. It was hard to resist shooting out some of the street lights by that old field. But I knew if I abused the privilege my gun days would be over for a while."

Then Nick looked at me across the lunch table and asked, "Why are you asking me these things about guns, anyway?"

He still hadn't made the connection. Nick had been trained how to teach a child about guns, but he had no background on dating training. To him it was obvious that there was an important training process for the guns, but he was oblivious as to what to do about dating. Nick's case is not unusual. Generations ago there was a slow-moving process called courting. And courting was only in the cultures that allowed the young people any decisions at all. In many other cultures the parents just picked who the young people would marry. There was no courting.

Courting was a process that had rules. The parents were obligated to incorporate this dating process step by step. Today's parents are the ones who didn't grow up under the courting procedure. Hence they are left without any idea as to what to do about the way their children enter into dating.

"I asked you about guns because I happen to already know that you have a plan for the way you trained your son about the use of a shotgun. I heard you talking about it in Bible study the other night. As important as you believe it is to have a plan to teach your son about guns, don't you think it's even more important to have a plan for dating? You wouldn't just hand a child a gun and say, 'Have fun.' Why are you doing that with dating?"

I'll never forget Nick looking at me and nodding in agreement. Then with a smile he said, "You know, you're right, but when you first asked me if my son had a gun, for a split second I thought you were going to suggest that we use it on Pam's boyfriend!"

A PLAN FOR DATING

The previous chapter discussed the importance of having a plan for selecting a spouse, it's equally important to have a plan for the progression of the whole dating process. How else will young people know what to do? Pam is not a rebellious young lady. She's just doing what she thinks people dating are supposed to be doing. She sees her parents sitting in the family room, Mom in Dad's lap, kissing. That's okay for a married couple, but not appropriate for Pam. She's been left to her own to decide what's supposed to happen on dates. That's very dangerous.

Many young people will get their dating information from the television sitcoms. Watching the way the precocious teens on television date, flaunt their sexuality, and act overly promiscuous is far from the way our teens need to be interacting with each other. But without a plan and ongoing discussion, how will they know? Just as the handing over of the gun was a deliberate and thoughtful series of actions, dating too needs to be prepared for and taken seriously.

SET THE AGENDA AHEAD OF TIME

"When will I be able to date?" is the question on many teens' lips. It's a question that is asked by many, long before they are in their teens or even interested. Some teens want the confidence of knowing that their parents have a plan. Asking the question forces the parent to verbalize a plan.

Unfortunately, many parents are unprepared for this question. Instead of giving an actual age as to when the teen will be able to date, they abdicate their parental leadership in this area. When asked this question, my friend had said to his daughter Pam, "We'll cross that bridge when we come to it." When Pam asked what that meant, her father said that he would let her know if she could date when she was asked out. In other words, when a young man asked her out he would then tell her if she was old enough. That was a challenge. Pam now had to get herself asked out in order to find out if she could go out. This father set himself up for an ongoing debate with his daughter. She had to just keep asking. He didn't do that with a shotgun. Why would he do it with dating?

Long before a child passes into the teen years, the parents need to have established and announced several issues concerning dating. The first issue is the age when dating will be permissible.

SET THE AGE

Just as the issue of what movies a child should be permitted to see varies widely from family to family, the exact age when a teen should be permitted to start dating is debatable. As an example, not necessarily as a rule for every family to follow however (some teens aren't even mature enough at sixteen), our home has used the age of sixteen as a time for our teens to be permitted to start dating. It was announced to each child, no matter the gender. Yes, there were debates and statements made such as "I'm the only one in the whole school who's not allowed to date yet!" A statement that the teen probably does believe, but is far from accurate.

Whatever age is set needs to be one that the child learns you are confident in, to avoid ongoing arguments. The age needs be established

An appropriate age for dating needs be established because there are still other parameters that need to be defined.

because there are still other parameters that need to be defined. Definitions, such as what actually constitutes a date, will be debated.

Is a party where both genders are in attendance a date or a social event? Each parent has to make that determination and then add it to their definition. Along with establishing the age for dating, the progression of the dating experience will need to be discussed. There are two very basic issues here. One involves the actual events of the dates themselves. The second involves the sexual training. The extremely important sexual issues will be discussed in a separate chapter.

PROGRESSION CAN HELP KEEP THEM OUT OF THE BACKSEAT

Many teens find themselves in hot water during their first few dating experiences, because no one set guidelines. Let's assume that sixteen is the age when a teen will be permitted to begin dating. What kind of dating will that teen be permitted to do? Sound like an unnecessary question? What about the sixteen-year-old girl who is invited by a senior to the prom? Will she be able to go? Will she be permitted to go to the all-night party at the local hotel? "But Mom, it's the prom! Everybody stays there all night!" These questions need to be answered even before they are asked. (Not that that will stop the teen from asking them!)

Step One: Check It Out

Parties that are checked out ahead of time by calls to the host parent are a great way to start the interaction process. Some parents will want to let their teen participate in these parties before their sixteenth birthday as a way of practicing the interaction. "You're not going to call the parents again, are you?" the teen will undoubtedly ask. The parents need to show the teen just how precious he or she is to the family by affirming that a call will be made. "Of course I'm going to call. Let me ask you something. Do you think I'd let a perfect stranger borrow my car for the evening? If someone called and asked to use my car, even if I knew them, you wouldn't expect me to just say 'sure' without asking questions, would you? Of course not. That would be ridiculous. Do you think that I consider my car to be more valuable than you are? Of course I'm going to call and ask questions before they borrow *you* for the evening."

Step Two: Group Dating

Many church youth groups offer the opportunity for young people to go places in large groups. The kids aren't necessarily paired off, though inevitably some will be. This activity will once again help a young person practice cross-gender interaction.

From non-paired-off activities, the next step in the practice dating process is for the teen to be restricted to double dates only. A good rule of thumb is for the teen to be told that he or she can begin dating, but at first, it will only be double dating. That helps, though it certainly doesn't assure that a teen won't end up in a backseat.

Along with the double-date policy comes several other variables. First, the curfew. Curfew is once again something that should be set ahead of time. The raising and lowering of the time that a teen is due back at the house can be adjusted according to the way the whole dating scenario is being handled.

> *The raising and lowering of the time that a teen is due back at the house can be adjusted according to the way the whole dating scenario is being handled.*

"I'm the only one who has to be in at eleven o'clock on Friday nights. You only let me go out on dates one night a weekend. When can I get my curfew extended? I always have to leave the parties first."

The response to that last question can be one that places the responsibility back on the teen. "When you have gone on ten dates where you show us that you can handle that curfew responsibly by being home on time, then we'll talk about changing it to 11:30."

◄◦►

Clear boundaries need to be set: If the location has not yet been approved, it is off limits.

◄◦►

Be prepared for the gasp. "A half hour! That's all?" The fact that the teen acts like he wants the moon or 1:00 A.M. should not surprise a parent. Teens are excellent negotiators, always pushing for more. That's only smart. It's also part of their emancipation process. But parents need to respond with a responsible progression. This is a practice time. Remember my friend when he taught his son about that shotgun. He didn't step from letting the young man hold the gun in the garage and then say, "All right. Have fun. Take that gun out there, and we'll see you in the morning." It was a slow progression. Significantly slower than his son had wished.

The second variable to be discussed is a list of permissible destinations for dates. Where are they allowed to go? Where are they not allowed to go? These are questions that need to be answered, though a young person will constantly be asking about new, yet to be researched locations. Clear boundaries need to be set: If the location has not yet been approved, it is off limits.

"You didn't tell me I couldn't go there," Barbara protested when she told her parents where she had been that evening. "No, Barbara, you're right," her father responded. "But we didn't tell you that that was a place you *could* go, and that's the plan we're working with. If we haven't yet approved it, call us and ask. Otherwise, it's not one of the approved areas."

Discussions about movies and movie ratings, homes where the parents are not in the house, and so forth can help a teen avoid a significant amount of difficulty. They not only help the teen begin to understand the plan but also help avoid some of the difficult arguments. A key phrase here is "help avoid" some of the parent/teen arguing. It is the teen job to push for more. We should expect it. More significantly, it is the parent's job and responsibility to have a plan of action where dating is concerned. We must think through the boundaries.

Step Three: Dating Alone

When the teen is ready to be alone on a date, there are still many parameters to be set. There are still curfews, questions about the destinations of the evening events, and most significantly, questions to be answered about the other teen. This is where a parent needs to become interactive in the dating process. Parents need to meet the teen that their young person is going out with.

"What!" Laury screamed. "You want him to what? You want him to come over to our house and meet you before I can go out with him? I knew you had always said that that was what would have to happen. I guess I just didn't believe it would actually come to this."

After Laury had calmed down, while she was sitting at the kitchen table with her parents, her dad continued. "If you want to go out with this young man, you can have him over Sunday afternoon, so we can talk to him for a while. Just to get to know him."

It's a must that parents meet and get to know the young people that their teens date. For a son, it's just as easy for him to go to the girl's house, meet her parents, and then come by his own house, so his parents can meet the girl he is going to take out. By doing this, parents can do a great job of advising a teen on the people they are dating. Often the advice comes too late, however. After the teen has been dating a girl for four months and they are very emotionally involved, it's too late for the teen to be able to hear things objectively.

"But what if he doesn't want to come over here to meet you guys?" a desperate daughter asked.

"Well, honey," the parent explained, "if he doesn't want to come over here to spend a little time meeting us, then he obviously doesn't want to spend an evening with the most precious thing we have. He will have to decide how much he wants to go on a date with you. Don't worry, we won't scare him away. All we want to do is get to know who he is. We won't fingerprint and mug shot him!"

PARAMETERS OF ACCEPTABILITY

There are many other questions that parents must deal with and discuss. Again, these questions are handled best when they don't yet have a name and face attached to them, when the teen is not yet emotionally involved with one specific person. Questions such as "Will Christian teens be permitted to date non-Christian teens?" are easier to discuss when there isn't yet a non-Christian teen in the picture.

Try to say yes on the issues that seem to be in the gray areas. That will help, because there are so many other areas where saying no is mandatory.

Questions concerning date locations, acceptable movies, appropriate gifts to give and receive, and countless others will come up and should be discussed. Try to say yes on the issues that seem to be in the gray areas. That will help, because there are so many other areas where saying no is mandatory.

These discussions, though sometimes painful, will help the teen begin to develop discernment about the dating process. Discernment that will play a big part in how they make dating decisions when they are by themselves on a college campus. Will they be rebellious when away from home because they weren't allowed to discuss the decisions being made? Or will they be discerning because they understand the wisdom behind the process? Much of that depends on the way the discussions are handled. The teen must be allowed to talk.

The teen needs help establishing these guidelines and also in learning the thinking process behind the guidelines. It's up to the parents to help the child understand why it's important for Christians to date Christians. Teens need to know that parents are not religious bigots but are relying on the biblical concept of common ground. The vast differences between the lifestyle, expectations, and focus of commitment of a non-Christian and a Christian are just too wide a gulf. There's a reason not to be unequally yoked. It's not in the best interest of either party. It's a biblical mandate that needs to be discussed. And we do marry who we date. That too is a fact.

DATE WRAP-UPS

Parents should be in the habit of reviewing the dates from which their teens have just returned. That might be immediately after the date or the next day. These are not times for interrogations but rather times to ask just enough questions to offer the *teen* a time to ask questions. Painful experiences will be fresh on the teen's mind, and the opportunity to share them with a listening parent can be one of the most bonding experiences a parent and teen can have. For these opportunities to open up, a parent will need to be very patient. Teens will find it difficult to blurt out a dating failure unless they think the parent is truly interested.

Many parents will have to work hard at not playing detective, asking too many probing questions. If the teen wants to talk and feels that the parent is genuinely interested, details will eventually flow—often more details than a parent wants to hear!

DATE THEM YOURSELF

"I learned about going out on dates," one counselor in our office said. "And I especially learned about how I should be treated on dates by going out on 'dates' with my father. Once a month my dad and I would go out together. Sometimes it would be to dinner and sometimes to a movie or even a play. On some dates we would even dress up. My dad took each of his daughters out on dates and we each learned how to be treated like a lady."

Dads can do a lot for their daughters by setting up times to take them out. Starting early in life, pre-teen daughters can begin to look forward to a regular time alone on a "date" with Dad. Who better than Dad can teach his daughter how to begin to identify whether or not she is being treated like a lady. Some young girls don't know any better because they've never been treated any better. Taking a daughter out on a date can be a time of cultural expansion, as well as a time of great communication. It can also be a time of learning how to be treated properly by a date.

Moms can and should do the very same thing. A mom should set up times when she can be "taken out" on a date by her son. This is a time to teach him how to hold doors as well as how to pay a bill at a restaurant. How else will a boy know how to do these things unless he is taught? By dating her sons, Mom has an opportunity to teach her sons a respect for the opposite sex. Of course, this can be more difficult in homes where the father refuses to do the very things Mom is trying to teach. It needs to be a concerted effort on the part of both parents. By dating our children we can allow them time to practice dating with instructors.

NO ONE TOLD HER

Diane was sitting in my office. At twenty-eight years old, she was telling her dating story. "I started dating in high school and I was pretty much on my own. I was a good kid, so my parents let me decide what to do and not to do. My senior year I began dating a guy and we got very serious. My parents never met him until we had been dating for over a year. Then they became alarmed. I was eighteen and he was twenty-seven.

"Somehow our dating relationship progressed to the point where he controlled my every move. In fact, I even quit college for a year and moved in with him. I started this relationship without any real dating experience and no one to talk to about it. I guess my parents would have talked to me, but I didn't know how to open the conversation with them. Even though I probably would have pushed them away at first, I wish they had been more aggressive in helping to manage my dating life. I just didn't know anything about dating. No one gave me any guidelines. I never had practice. Over a period of eighteen months I got to the place where I just did whatever he told me to do. It got so bizarre that I lost my whole identity and basically became his sex slave. Finally I ran away and started over."

Years later this attractive young woman was sitting in a counselor's office talking about the fact that she was afraid to date anyone because of that disaster she had been through.

Guidelines might have prevented this horror story. Parental involvement could have stopped it before it progressed to a point where it changed a girl's life. Teenage boys and girls need their parents to be involved in their dating process more than anything else they do during their teenage years. Don't just cut them loose. Figuratively speaking, that's like cutting their throats. Develop a plan before you develop a problem.

SUMMARY

1. Before a child becomes a teenager, a parent needs to start thinking about the plan that will be implemented to ease into the dating process.
2. The dating progression needs to include variables such as the age when dating will begin, the kind of dating that will be permitted, and who the teen will be permitted to date.
3. Each person a teen dates should be required to meet the parents.
4. This is not a one lecture process but an ongoing discussion.

QUESTIONS

1. How old does your teen have to be before he or she can begin dating?
2. What is the dating progression that you feel best serves your child? Remember, we don't let them start learning to drive a car on the turnpike at sixty miles an hour. We use the safer, slower back roads. Don't start them dating at a speed that they can't possibly handle, even though they think they can.
3. What will be your policy about meeting the boy or girl that your teen wants to go out with?
4. What are the rules about dating locations?

Chapter Eleven

————◄◦►————

They're Watching

A re your parents going to be home?" sixteen-year-old Darla asked our daughter. Darla was coming over to spend Friday night at our house.

"Why?" Torrey asked.

"'Cause the last time I spent the night we played 'Gestures' with your parents. That was a riot."

The night Darla had stayed at our home, the two girls had talked into the morning hours. After Darla went home, Torrey said, "You know, Darla's parents never do anything with the kids. She said that they all go into their own rooms after dinner and either watch separate televisions or spend the night on the phone. Darla has to call one of her friends to have someone to talk to. They never all sit in their family room and talk or play games. She said that they even go on separate vacations. In the summer the kids go to camp while the parents go on a trip. Darla thought it was so different that you guys wanted to be with us."

Imagine a home where you have to use the telephone in order to have someone to talk to. Imagine a home where everyone is just too busy to sit and talk.

ENTERTAINMENT WAS FAMILY

Before having a television in every bedroom was a common practice, yesterday's child grew up in a home where the family's entertainment was generally the family. They sat at the dinner table for what used to be called the dinner hour. Today it's more like the dinner fifteen minutes. And that fifteen minutes is not even spent sitting at a table facing each other. Often it's at a TV table in front of the television. Nobody talks, they just watch. Or they eat in shifts, alone, because not everyone is home at the same time.

At the dinner hour, yesterday's child not only talked but listened, having the opportunity to watch parents interact and make decisions. Families even did dishes together and played games after dinner. Or they'd read together in the "sitting room" or "parlor." Or they'd end the day sitting on the porch to catch a breeze if the weather was hot or adjourn to the coziness of the fireplace if it was cool. Children were part of the family, able to be with their parents, coached by their parents.

Yesterday's child grew up in a home where the family's entertainment was generally the family.

The very nature of the interdependent lifestyle of the past afforded children further opportunities to watch and be with their parents. Many families all worked together. Children learned about marriage primarily from their parents, seeing how their parents worked through the difficulties that come with marriage.

No, we can't turn the clocks back. We can't live the way our grandparents and great-grandparents used to live. What we can do is be aware that many of today's children are learning about marriage from role models who are not family members. The marriage that many of today's children grow up watching appears in front of them on the television set. These are often incredibly demeaning marriages of the sitcoms. Many of the relationships viewed on television make fun of the male role model, degrade the sexual relationship, or present a female role that is crass and foul. This generation of children is growing up not only laughing at these sitcoms, but knowing more about these television marriages than they know about their own parents' marriage. That's because they spend more time watching these fictitious husbands and wives interacting than they do watching their own parents interact.

The typical television marriage portrays an atmosphere of self-centeredness where each spouse must battle to get his or her needs met. Rarely does the viewer get to see the sacrificial attitude necessary for a growing, vibrant, real-life marriage. By the mere nature of the one-hour program, the media marriage also leaves the impression that all problems can be worked out in sixty (or thirty) minutes. Not only is this unrealistic, but it tends to leave a person (not only impressionable young persons) with very damaging expectations when it comes to real life.

Concerning role models, these questions need to be answered: What marriage does the typical child of today see most often? Busy parents, interacting at home or the various television marriages viewed during the 22,000 hours of television the average child watches before the age of eighteen? Couples would do well to rethink their schedules, if for no other reason than to "be married" in front of their children.

THOSE NONVERBAL LESSONS

Every December, while I was growing up, my dad had a tradition he maintained with his sons. One Saturday early in the month he would take us into New York City to shop and eat lunch. It was a two-stop trip. One stop was fun and the other was always a nightmare for my brother and me. The day would end with a trip to a special hamburger restaurant where we sat around a huge counter and watched our order delivered on the flatbed of a Lionel train. It stopped right in front of where we were sitting. It was awesome!

Before we got to go to the Choo Choo Burger, however, we had to endure going with Dad into Macy's to get my mother her annual Christmas nightgown. Definitely not for young boys. My dad would take us into the lingerie section, where we would die a thousand deaths. And he twisted the knife, too. "What do you think, boys?" he'd ask, holding a nightgown up next to him. We just knew that anyone in Macy's lingerie who witnessed this annual scene was sure Dad was buying it for himself. "Just get it and get out of here, Dad," we would beg.

Those were very embarrassing Saturdays for us, but he made them a priority every year. The pain of the lingerie nightmare was almost (and I do stress the word "almost") compensated for by the trip to the Choo Choo Burger.

Many years later Rosemary and I were sitting in front of the Christmas tree at our own home, just talking. We had been married for a few years and it was the evening of Christmas day. We had unwrapped the gifts that morning and we were reviewing the Christmas season. As I watched Rosemary, I could tell something was on her mind, but she wasn't saying what it was. "I missed something this Christmas, didn't I?" I said.

"No," she immediately protested. "Everything was wonderful!"

But I knew better. Christmas married to a German can be very boring. The gifts tend to have utilitarian meaning. Monogrammed towels, assorted kitchen tools, and other matter-of-fact gifts. Knowing that there was definitely something on her heart, I continued to push and she finally said, "It was a great Christmas. But I guess if I could add one thing that I would have liked to receive, it would be something that would show me that I was still sexy to you. You know. . .a nightgown or something."

When Rosemary said "nightgown," I felt like a lightbulb had exploded in my head. That was it! That was what Dad was doing! He wasn't taking us with him because the Choo Choo Burger just happened to be near Macy's. He had a purpose in the midst of all that embarrassment. It was to teach his boys about being a husband.

I guess he could have just sat us down and told us that when we grew up, it would be good to remember to buy our wives nightgowns. But who would have listened? Certainly not me! At thirteen I would have thought that a disgusting suggestion. Furthermore, I would have had no idea how to go about it. Instead of telling us, he gave us a visual aid to remember and walk us through the process. He was taking the time to teach us how to be husbands. But it took Rosemary to complete the lesson.

The example we set for our children is based on the marriage we saw in our parents' home. And our children's marriage will be based on the marriage that they see in our home. Parents need to ask themselves:

- What example are we setting?
- What are our children getting to see walked out in the day-to-day laboratory of our marriage?
- Who is supplying our children with examples of the marriage relationship?

A PRIORITY

Children need to see that their parents believe that the marriage relationship is a priority. Keeping your marriage a priority will be, and should be, an ongoing struggle when you combine busy schedules with the demands of children. The children will constantly want to be a part of the marriage relationship. They will even want to be a part of the master bedroom bed. They should be able to spend time with us, but every now and then they should hear us say, "Mom and I need to have some time to ourselves tonight." That lets them "hear" by our actions that our marriage is important.

Children need to see that their parents believe that the marriage relationship is a priority.

When our daughter Torrey was fifteen, it became apparent that she no longer needed a bedtime. Month after month, we slowly stretched her bedtime further and further into the evening, finally making it contingent on her being able to get up in the morning without a problem. When she showed us that this was a personal responsibility she could handle, we told her she no longer had a specific bedtime. She could go to bed whenever she wanted to. It was her decision, provided she was able to get up at 6:00 A.M. and get ready for school without complaining or dragging around the house.

This was a great way to put personal responsibility in her hands, except there was one problem. Rosemary and I found that we no longer had any time alone as a couple. Torrey thought that since she got to stay up as late as we did, that we should always be available to do things with her. She acted as if it was our job to entertain her. Finally, one night I announced to her, "At nine o'clock you need to head on up to your room."

"Why?" she protested. "You said I don't have a bedtime anymore. Why do I have to go to bed at nine?"

"You don't have to go to bed at nine," I said. "You just can't be downstairs after nine. Mom and I need a little time in front of the fireplace alone tonight."

With that Torrey mischievously asked, "Well, what would happen if I came downstairs after nine?"

I'm sure she didn't expect my response. "If you come downstairs after nine o'clock, you will probably find two naked bodies in front of the fireplace!" Torrey turned beet red!

Why would I say that to my daughter? For two reasons. One was the fact that I didn't want her coming downstairs! But the more important reason was that I wanted my daughter to know that I adore her mother and love spending time alone with her. The passion portrayed on television is nowhere near as beautiful as the passion that her mother and I share. Passion is for married couples and I want her to know it. Not being an exhibitionist, I felt the only way she would know it was if we made reference to it. She needed to know that I love her mom! And we want to be an endorsement of an exciting marriage.

Though many kids might act like they feel rejected when they are told that "mom and dad need to go out alone tonight," in reality it accomplishes two very important things. It helps them to feel secure about their parents' marriage in a time when marriage seems so fragile. It also teaches them how to establish their own priorities for marriage time. Life is very demanding. The last thing to be given time in our schedules is often the marriage relationship. Many fail to schedule in "marriage time" simply because they don't know how to do it. They never saw it done. It will help the marriages of our children if they see how we allocate our time and put a priority on "marriage time."

TEACHING BY DEMONSTRATION

The way spouses deal with each other teaches much about a relationship. The attitudes that one spouse conveys about another spouse teaches a child lessons. How a husband reacts to an opinion of his wife teaches whether or not men are supposed to respect the opinions of women. The attitudes we learn in the home are not only carried into our marriage, they're carried into the workplace.

Sitting in our homes are future husbands and wives who are observing the way their parents deal with conflict. When a disagreement takes place, is there a discussion or is there an eruption of anger? Do the children see conflict handled through an atmosphere of mutual respect or with exploding rage? Or with slammed doors and silence? Or with violence? We are teaching them how to handle conflict by the way we handle conflict. And as we all know, marriage includes a major amount of conflict.

> *Sitting in our homes are future husbands and wives who are observing the way their parents deal with conflict.*

But did we know before we got married that conflict is part of the marriage relationship? Many young people grow up in homes that have the policy that parents should never disagree in front of the children. What does that do for the children? Not much. In fact, it gives them a distorted image of what the marriage relationship is all about. It doesn't give them the opportunity to watch how two people who love each other handle those inevitable disagreements.

"I thought that two people who were in love and got married would have everything in common," Elizabeth said through her tears. "I mean, I knew we'd have things that we disagreed on. I just didn't know they could become such big issues. I just never saw my parents fight like we do. Now that I think about it, I never saw my parents disagree about anything. My dad just decided and my mom agreed. But I can't do that. I have a brain too. It just seems like Bobby doesn't want me to use it unless it agrees with his."

Conflict resolution is a needed skill in marriage. Later chapters in this book explore how to prepare our children to handle money and deal with their sexual relationship—typical areas of conflict in a marriage. The primary difficulty, however, is not money or sex, but how spouses choose to disagree about these areas. The way we discuss the disagreements is the key.

It's important that the children growing up in our homes realize that it's okay to have a different opinion. It's important for them to see that the right to those opinions will be respected. It's even more important for them to be able to watch us resolve conflicts so that they can learn to resolve the conflicts that are inevitable for them to face.

PARTICIPATING IN DISCUSSIONS OF CONFLICTS

There are two ways for children to learn skills in the area of conflict resolution. One way children learn conflict resolution is for parental discussions to occur behind closed doors. Children then learn to fear disagreement. Their immature thinking leads them to believe that either there is no conflict or that it must be so terrible that Mom and Dad don't dare resolve it in front of them. Their conflict resolution skills amount to simple avoidance.

The other way is for the children to be able to observe adults resolving conflicts in a respectful manner. Parental differences of opinion handled at the dinner table can be very instructive. These discussions teach children that disagreement between two people who love each other is not a bad thing: Even though Mom and Dad disagree, they don't stop loving each other. Children also learn that differences can be handled in a loving, respectful way. They learn what compromise is as they see the give and take of a healthy and perhaps lively discussion. They learn that resolving conflict is far less uncomfortable than allowing it to fester.

Our daughter, Torrey, had asked her mom if she could go with her friends to a party on Friday night.

Rosemary's response was, "Let's ask your dad."

To which Torrey responded, "Oh, he'll just say no. He always says no."

"Torrey, you know I can't say yes without first talking to your dad." This was an opportunity to teach our daughter that spouses make decisions together. But there was still another lesson to be played out for our fifteen-year-old. "Let's ask your dad at dinner."

That night Rosemary said, "Torrey has something she wants to ask us." That kind of opening line always scares me to death. After saying that, Rosemary looked at Torrey.

She said, "George is having his birthday party at a country club this weekend and I got invited. Can I go?"

Torrey was right. My first inclination is always to say no. It just seems safer for a dad. I don't know why I'm like that, but, sure enough, it came out of my mouth. "No, I don't think so, honey."

To which Torrey responded, "Can we discuss it?"

My gut-level response to a question like that is "No, we can't discuss it!" But I know that's wrong. She was acting more like an adult than I was. This was more than just a discussion about a party, it was an opportunity to teach her to talk and deal with differences of opinion without yelling or throwing a temper tantrum. We had an opportunity to teach her about conflict resolution.

I asked Rosemary what her thoughts were on the party, and it became apparent that we had mildly different opinions. Torrey sat back and watched as we discussed our thoughts and feelings about her going to the party. She was able to hear our concerns as well as the way we respected each other's opinions. She also took part in the discussion.

"Torrey," I said, as we finished the dinner table discussion, "let me think about it until bedtime. Mom and I will keep talking. But I want you to know that you have done a great job of keeping your cool during this discussion. The real test, however, will be when you get our answer. If it's not the answer that you want, will you still be able to show this kind of maturity or will you stomp off in a tantrum? That will be the test. Thanks for talking about this in such a mature way."

SIBLING RIVALRY — PRACTICE FOR MARRIAGE

Today's child has very little that he or she has to share with anyone. Sharing opens up yet another door of opportunity for dealing with conflict. Yesterday's family had a few family toys. Today's family has closets full of separate toys for each child. Yesterday's child borrowed the family bicycle when someone else wasn't using it. Today's children get on their own bicycle and become angry if anyone else has touched it. Yesterday's child often shared a bed with siblings. Today's child doesn't even share a bedroom.

> *Any parenting plan needs to include ways for children to practice disagreeing agreeably.*

The operative word for yesterday's child was "ours." The key word for today's child is "mine!" No wonder it's difficult for children to learn to negotiate and compromise. No wonder it's hard for young adults to learn to deal with differences of opinion. They've never practiced sharing. They haven't had an opportunity to learn to handle the conflicts that are inevitable with sharing. No wonder it's hard for them to stay married.

Once again, we can't go back to yesterday, but we can teach the lessons that were taught yesterday. The children of today might not have to share as much, but we can put them into situations where they will have to learn to share some things and learn to compromise.

Randy got tired of battling with his two children every time they were in the car. "Can we stop and get a Coke, Dad?" "Can we go through the drive-through and get a milk shake?" It seemed like they were nickeling and diming him to death. It didn't end there. Every weekend the children were asking to order a pizza and rent a video. Then they would want to get a hamburger and french fries. Money wasn't the issue; Randy was financially secure. The issue was that he was always put in the position of deciding whether they were going to buy a treat or not. He was the one who had to say no. He was concerned that his children weren't making the decision for themselves. All they were learning was to ask. They weren't learning to share or compromise when they couldn't agree on what to get. Randy decided to change that.

"From now on," Randy announced at the dinner table one night, "you two are going to be the ones who decide whether we're going to be able to order a pizza, get a soda at the drive-through, or get a video." Vickie and Brian were all ears. "On the first and fifteenth of each month I'm going to put thirty-five dollars in this jar," Randy said, holding up the jar. "We're going to leave this jar down here in the kitchen. When it's empty, that's it. No more sodas until the next payday. When one of you asks if we can rent a video, all I will say is, 'Is there enough money in the jar?'"

That seemed like a great idea to Vickie and Brian; thirty-five dollars was a lot of money. Then a problem arose and Randy almost canceled the whole idea. Driving home from church one evening, Vickie asked if they could go through the drive-through and get sodas. Randy asked her if there was enough money in the jar at home and she said there was still fourteen dollars. As he was preparing to turn in, Brian protested. "No! I don't want to get sodas now! If we do, there won't be any money left to rent *Jungle Book* this weekend. It's just coming out on video and we won't be able to see it!"

It appeared to be a real dilemma. Randy didn't know what to do. Instead of pulling over, he just kept driving and the kids kept arguing. Once they were home, Randy felt like his plan had been shown to be a dismal failure. "It didn't work," Randy said to his wife.

"I disagree. I think it worked perfectly. We put that financial decision in their hands and they saw how difficult it can be. Now we'll tell them that before the money can be spent, they both have to agree on how to spend it. They have to learn to deal with their differences. They'll have to learn to share that one pot. Tonight they sounded like an old married couple. In fact, they sounded like we did when we first got married and I wanted the new carpeting and you wanted the bass boat, and we couldn't buy both. This is going to be great practice for when they get married."

Any parenting plan needs to include ways for children to practice disagreeing agreeably. They will need practice in conflict resolution. They need to see it done properly by their parents, and then they need to be put into a "laboratory setting" so they can work on these skills themselves. Sure it's easier for parents to avoid the hassles and just give the kids what they want. But that guarantees a more difficult adult life for them. Because life isn't free of conflict. Marriage isn't free of conflict. Children need to grow up with the skills to handle conflicts and disagreements.

Sibling rivalry can't be avoided, but it can be put to great use. It's a perfect opportunity for practicing marriage. Instead of getting a television for every room, teach your children how to discuss what they're going to watch on the one television in the family room.

BUT WHAT ABOUT THE SINGLE PARENT?

"All this sounds real nice," a woman said at a seminar, "but what about those of us who are single moms? What are we supposed to do about role models?"

There's no instant answer for that question. Rather than sounding flippant about the plight of the single parent by inserting a few sentences here, let me say that I've devoted a whole book on the topic. In *Single Parenting* I constantly stressed that no one should agonize over or attempt to do things that are impossible to do. A single parent can't model a marriage. Instead, focus your energies on the things that can be done. Though the single parent will not be able to model the marriage relationship, there are things he or she can model concerning handling relationships.

The single parent can work on setting a good example in two basic areas of relationships. One area of relationship that is very important is the way the single parent talks about his or her ex-spouse. Though there might be many dramatic differences of opinion between the two estranged spouses, they are still the parents of the children. The way one spouse talks about the other will be a crucial lesson for the children to observe.

"Do you mean to say," a single parent cut in, "that if my ex makes nasty comments about me to the children I should just ignore them?"

That's exactly what I mean to say. The fact that one spouse responds in an immature way is certainly no license for the other spouse to do the same. Two immature parents will teach the children how to resolve conflicts in an immature manner. One mature parent responding to life's conflicts in a mature manner can show the children an alternative way of dealing with differences of opinion. The greater the contrast in attitudes, the greater the illustration.

It was a similar situation that had a great impact on my own life and attitude. In 1966 I arrived on a college campus, very bitter due to the death of my mother. In my anger, I met and began seeing a girl on our campus who was a strong Christian. She refused to take part in my bitter comments about life. In fact, she was very positive about life. At the end of that year, one of the nation's most outspoken atheists came to lecture at our campus. Expecting to hear some profound wisdom, I went to her lecture series, only to be shocked by this speaker's own bitterness. It permeated the entire lecture. The girl I had been dating was sitting next to me at the end of one of the lectures, and as I looked over at her the contrast became startling. One person was bitter and angry like me. The other was hopeful and positive about life. I wanted the hope that she had. I took her by the hand, walked her out of the lecture, and asked her what it was that made her so full of joy. "The very same thing that the lecturer has rejected is what brings me joy," she said. "My faith in Christ."

It was her joy and refusal to be brought down by negative attitudes that changed my life. She was positive and had hope. The contrast with the speaker was impossible to miss. In fact, that contrast caused me to spend the next five years working at getting Rosemary to marry me.

The single parent should not get trapped in the game of negatives and accusations. You can't control your ex, but you can control the way you talk about your ex. That's your choice.

The single parent can also model conflict resolution by the way differences of opinion are handled in the home. Are the children allowed to express their opinions when they differ from yours? Granted, that's often exhausting, but it's also very instructional. A significant marriage skill is to learn how to disagree agreeably. No one knows that better than a single parent.

STEPPARENTS

Can a stepparent marriage do role modeling? There is probably no greater opportunity for teaching than in the stepparent home. Perhaps the children watched a bitter divorce. The way the new marriage is handled will teach them about a positive marriage. The discussions that need to take place in every stepparent marriage can be very instructional to the children who are trying to learn, all over again, about marriage and family. Stepparents have the same opportunities as natural parents, only there might be more urgency in the blending family. (These issues and others are discussed in my book *You're Not My Daddy*.)

SUMMARY

1. We need to realize that we are the most significant marriage our children will see. They learn much by watching us.
2. Our marriage teaches the next generation about conflict resolution and about marriage as a priority in life by the way we schedule our marriage time.
3. Sibling rivalry is great practice for marriage.
4. Yes, Torrey did get to go to the party!

QUESTIONS

1. How can you change your schedule to spend more time as a family, time when your children get to see you interact as a couple?
2. How can you encourage your children to disagree with you in an agreeable manner? Do they ever hear their parents discuss a decision when the parents have differing opinions?
3. Do the children have any area of their lives where they must work together to make a decision? Areas might be involve activities, what shows to watch, what videos to rent, or how to spend the entertainment money.
4. What's the most important positive trait your children would learn by observing your marriage? What negative trait?

Chapter Twelve

————◄◇►————

Purposeful Communication

"We don't talk anymore" is the number-one complaint of wives.

"Oh, how we talked when we were dating," Nancy piped in. "We sat out in front of my dorm for hours and talked. Then we got married and that was it. The conversation stopped. If I want to talk about something more important than which one of us is going to pick up the kids from practice, he has nothing to say."

In an age of what we like to refer to as high-tech communication, we sure aren't communicating in the home. After more than twenty-five years of counseling, I hear three areas of marital dissatisfaction most frequently raised: lack of communication, conflicts over finances, and difficulty regarding sexual issues.

————◄◇►————

Couples lack the communication skills to deal with conflict.

————◄◇►————

In reality, all these issues probably boil down to one difficulty: Couples find it very difficult to communicate. Even the difficulties couples have with finances and sexual issues are due to the fact that they can't talk to each other about these issues. Couples lack the communication skills to deal with the conflicts that quite naturally arise in both the sexual and financial areas of a relationship.

Time is a factor that affects our communication. Communication is no longer a natural part of family activities. It's no longer part of family entertainment. Husbands and wives are caught up in separate jobs instead of meeting to discuss their family-owned business. But the lack of time is only an excuse. It's more than a time-management difficulty. We certainly have enough time to watch television. For the majority of spouses, it's a lack of understanding about the communication process. This lack of understanding of the "how to and why" of marital communication stems from a lack of training. If parents are truly concerned about the growth and success of their child's future marriage, then parents need to take on the task of teaching communication skills.

"Is all this really necessary?" you might ask. After reading more than halfway through this book, you might be saying to yourself, "Look, I can't believe that we need to teach our children how to communicate. How important is this, really?"

Several years ago, a man (let's call him Sam) was in my office lamenting the issue of communication. "I know this gets me into trouble," Sam confessed. "I don't know how to sit and talk to my wife for ten minutes, and yet I can talk to women at the office for hours. I enjoy talking to women. Talking to other women is at first exciting, and then the next thing I know I'm heading for trouble. If I could only learn to channel that communication back home."

> *One couple after another settles for a mediocre marriage simply because they don't know how to open the lines of communication.*

Another example is Susan. She was in a marriage where there was no longer any communication. She and her husband had stopped talking long ago. The fact that they had stopped talking didn't in any way mean that she no longer desired a relationship that included deep communication. In fact, she craved it, so much so that one December she found herself staying late after choir rehearsal, engaged in deep conversation with one of the men in the choir. She meant nothing by it, but found the communication with this other man to be intoxicating. Many nights they sat talking as late as they dared. Then she realized that this unfulfilled void in her life, this lack of communication in her marriage, had gotten her into trouble.

One final scenario is all too familiar, so familiar that it doesn't need any particular names attached. One couple after another settles for a mediocre marriage simply because they don't know how to open the lines of communication. They are determined to stay married even though the reality of marriage is hardly the marriage of depth they dreamed about. Instead of pushing to open the lines of communication and develop the relationship, they just settle—settle for decades of marital mediocrity because they didn't know how to do any differently.

Parents should want better than that for their children. Understanding that communication in marriage is often difficult, parents should do whatever they can to help prepare the child to succeed at this process. Training for successful communication is mandatory.

Communication is the "central nervous system" of the marriage relationship. It's the information giver and the feelings detector. When the communication process is not functioning, paralysis hits the marriage.

PREPARE THEM FOR THE PITFALLS

If we know ahead of time that there are difficulties our children will have to face later on in life, we would be derelict as parents not to try to do our best to prepare them. Why is it so difficult to prepare our children for good marital communication? One reason is that today's adults never observed the process. Chances are they didn't see their parents talk to each other. Chances are even better that the parents didn't spend much time talking with the children. Talking *to* children is not the same as talking *with* them.

Parents need to both teach their children how to talk and how to listen, and they need to demonstrate how it's done.

Obviously parents need to do two things. Parents need to both teach their children how to talk and how to listen, and they need to demonstrate how it's done. This is communication of more than just the weather. The growth of a relationship is directed by the ability to talk at a level that shares inner feelings. I firmly believe that when God said, "It is not good for the man to live alone," in Genesis 2, he then gave man a partner to help him learn how to open up and talk. Marriage was not meant to be primarily an arrangement where parents divide up the chores of who picks up which child when. Marriage was meant to be an enriching process of growing closer and closer by sharing thoughts and feelings. This is a very difficult process for people who don't know how to communicate.

"HOW CAN WE HAVE A RELATIONSHIP WITHOUT FEELINGS?"

Marie sat in the counselor's office, pouring her heart out. "Why is it I can have these discussions with you, a perfect stranger, and Mark and I can't talk like this?" She was looking at the counselor and sobbing over the fact that her husband seemed to be incapable of expressing any feeling at all. "Oh," she continued, getting sarcastic, "he can express feelings when those Gators lose a football game. Then he expresses feelings. But when it's just the two of us and I'm trying to talk to him about the way I feel, I might as well be talking to the lawnmower. He looks very uncomfortable and just can't respond. It's very frustrating. Doesn't having a real relationship mean that two people share their feelings?"

"I know that Mark has feelings," the counselor responded. "I was with him at the Promise Keepers conference this summer. After one of the speakers, Mark was so moved that he wept. I know it's in there, he just doesn't know how to get the feelings out and talk about them."

GIRLS HAVE PERMISSION

At a very early age, our culture permits girls to show a wide range of feelings. Many boys, on the other hand, are taught that it is only okay to show feelings of aggression or elation over a victory. Boys are taught to suppress their feelings of hurt when they are told, "Now, now, big boys don't cry." Then they are taught to express their feelings on the soccer or football field. "You need to get up for this game! You act like you don't care whether you win or lose! Come on, get pumped!"

As a result, it's more natural for girls to express a wide range of feelings than it is for boys. Girls in our culture relate to friends at a deeper level via their feelings and emotions. Boys relate to others, starting at an early age, via competition. First in line, first on the bus, first to be picked for the game—these are all very important in a young boy's relationships. He's been taught to compete for first.

The fact that girls seem to be more comfortable relating their feelings to others is further developed throughout their teenage years. Girls get on the phone and talk to their friends about who hurt whose feelings or about how bad they felt when they didn't get asked to go to the party. They enhance the development of the communication of feelings through the use of the telephone. The male population makes fun of the fact that the female gender spends so much time on the phone. But girls benefit from a real by-product of using the phone: They get a lot of time to "practice feelings."

Talking to someone about hurt feelings without having to look them in the eye is very freeing. Many people today use the telephone or even the Internet to practice relationships by communicating with people they have never met in person and hardly know. A daughter might get on the phone for forty-five minutes (or as long as she can get away with tying up the phone) and relate to a friend. A son will probably get on the phone for three minutes to ask questions about who won the game and who had the best play. That is, unless he's trying to develop a relationship with the opposite sex. Then the competitive juices to "win" the relationship kick in. The way to win this game of girlfriends is to talk and share. His time on the phone goes up.

A girl generally has the stronger desire to communicate feelings, plus she's had more practice through her teen years. She communicates with her date. Then she gets married, expecting the ultimate relationship of communication. Little wonder she's frustrated. Her husband has no idea what to do: He's totally unprepared.

Parents need to teach their children, especially their boys, how to communicate and express feelings. It's an essential part of the marriage relationship. She wants to share feelings, and he wonders what she's talking about. She says, "Tonight, can we just sit on the porch and talk?" He says, "Why?" and he really means it. She answers, "Because I have some things I want to share with you." He thinks to himself, "Why doesn't she just write them down and hand them to me? I'll read them and check them off. What's with this sharing stuff, anyway?"

> *There are many wives still waiting for their husbands to do things spontaneously. But how can he if he wasn't taught or told?*

Those who are married already know this is an area that needs work. With that in mind, we should be helping to prepare the next generation to be able to do a better job. We should be raising them to be able to develop the best marriage possible.

EXPRESSING EASY FEELINGS

Learning to express feelings should start with the communication of easy feelings. Feelings aren't always connected with pain or discomfort. Children at a young age can be taught the feeling of gratitude.

Many spouses indicate that they feel taken for granted, or just plain taken. "I can't believe that she says she feels that way. I appreciate her more than she could possibly know." A young husband exhaled in frustration.

"But have you ever told her?" he was asked.

"Of course I've shown her. I show her every day by the way I work to make her happy."

"I didn't say *show* her, I said *told* her. Have you ever said to her that you appreciate something specific that she does?"

"Like what, for instance?" was his reply. "What specifically should I say?"

In one minute, this young husband went from frustration to confusion. He knew he appreciated his wife. He now knew that she didn't *feel* appreciated. But he also knew that he didn't know how to express his appreciation verbally in a way that she would understand.

At an early age our children can be taught to overcome this difficulty. "From now on, children," a parent at the dinner table can explain, "before you leave the dinner table, you need to say to Mom, 'Thanks for dinner, Mom.' From now on we're going to show our appreciation for the fact that she goes to the trouble to make us dinner."

Are we doing that for Mom? Certainly some of it is for Mom. Mom deserves to be shown gratitude. More significantly, however, by stating our thanks to Mom we are teaching the children an attitude of gratitude (to use an overworked phrase). Gratitude is taught and caught. It's not genetic.

"Oh, I don't want to force them to thank me for the meal," one mother said. "If they think about it on their own that will be great, but I don't want to make it mandatory." She was thinking about it all wrong. It's not primarily for her. It's for the training. If she's waiting for them to spontaneously show appreciation, she'll be waiting a lifetime. So will the spouse of her children. There are many wives still waiting for their husbands to do things spontaneously. But how can he if he wasn't taught or told?

There are many times, every day, in the life of a family when one person does something for another. One child allows another child to sit in the much-coveted front seat of the car. (I know it's unusual, but it could happen.) A parent can start the ball of appreciation rolling by saying "thanks" to that child and then look at the other child.

The lesson starts with the action of requiring children to show appreciation. Later on the feelings of appreciation will follow, especially when appreciation is shown toward something they have done. "Billy, I want to thank you for taking the time to bring the paper in for me. Your thoughtfulness saved me the trip. I appreciate that very much. Thank you." Going overboard helps to make the point and set the example.

"But how do you get started?" a parent asked. For starters, make the announcement at the dinner table that everyone must express gratitude to Mom for the meal before they leave the table. Let them know that gratitude can be expressed in one of two ways, either verbally, saying thanks to Mom for the meal, or by writing it in a note directly after dinner. Every night. No exceptions. Those who don't say it will write it. It won't take long for positive statements to come out of their mouths.

"I hate to require them to write a note for not showing me gratitude," most overly sensitive mothers are thinking right now. Again, it's not only an expression for you. It's training that benefits their spouses. Your future daughter-in-law and son-in-law will thank you. Besides, no one ever has to write this note unless, of course, they refuse to learn to say, "Thanks for dinner, Mom." Not that difficult to learn and the benefits later on are worth it.

REMORSE

Another step in successful relationships is developing the maturity to feel and express remorse. Many adults feel sorry for something that has happened, but they fall short when it comes time to expressing remorse. The words "I'm sorry. Will you forgive me?" get stuck in their mouths.

Regardless of the popular line in the 1970s movie *Love Story,* "Love means never having to say you're sorry," a relationship of love most certainly does mean that a person must be able to say he or she is sorry. It's important to know how to say you're sorry and feel remorse. Again, that comes with training and with watching the trainers.

As parents, do we set the example by expressing the feeling of remorse to all the family members? Do the children see us apologize to each other? It's worth apologizing in front of the children. They learn the lesson. Do our

Do our children have parents willing to apologize to them when we are wrong? Such a lesson and demonstration will long be remembered.

children have parents willing to apologize to them when we are wrong? Such a lesson and demonstration will long be remembered. This demonstration says, "Mature adults are those who are able to admit they were wrong and ask for forgiveness." This expression of feelings is a vital ingredient in a growing marital relationship.

"But what about the fact that my children just blurt out, 'Sorry,' but obviously don't really mean it?"

Teaching the verbal response is the first step. There are many adults who feel sorry but can't say it. The second step is the ongoing process of teaching true remorse. That takes hours of sitting on a child's bed and helping the child understand another person's feelings. Use phrases such as, "How would you feel if . . ." Teach a child that just saying "sorry" isn't enough. Showing that you are truly sorry is the real task. That also means trying not to do it again.

This is a very important issue in our culture today. Today people are sorry only because they were caught in the act, not because they did something wrong. That's due to a lack of proper parenting. Feeling and expressing remorse is learned in a training process that begins when a parent requires the child to express remorse, then takes time to teach the reason for true feeling. "It seems like such a waste of time making them say it," a frustrated mom said. "Anyone can tell by the way they say it that they don't really mean it." But the lesson starts with the verbal expression. Later they will learn the emotion of being sorry. Many married partners have the emotion of remorse, but find it difficult to express it in words. Teach your children when they are still children to say they're sorry. That's the first step toward feeling remorse.

FEELINGS

Teaching a child about feelings takes time. Often it takes asking the right questions. Today's parents are "project oriented" rather than "feelings oriented." Both orientations are required.

Parents get into the routine of asking project-oriented questions, such as, "How was school today?" to which the child gives the obligatory answer, "Fine."

Next question from the parent, "What did you do today?"

To which the child has learned to respond, "Nothing."

The parent closes with, "Oh, okay. Do you want some juice before you start your homework?" End of conversation.

The dialogue of marriage isn't much different. The responses have become routine.

Feelings are deeper and take more time to come out. Bedtime is often one of the best times to help a child practice talking about feelings. Try sitting on the side of a child's bed, using feeling openers such as

- "How did it make you feel when your sister said that to you this afternoon?"
- "You know, Honey, when you said that about your lunch today, I want you to know that it hurt my feelings."
- "How did you think Larry felt when you . . ."
- "How did you feel when you didn't get picked?"

A child won't know how to respond to these deeper questions immediately. It is the parent's job to help the child find the right words. This process is not a three-minute "sit on the side of the bed" process. Nor is it for every night. It's for a time when something has happened that lends itself to staying in a child's room longer or going for a ride in the car to open the lines of communication between a child's heart and mouth.

The process of teaching a child to communicate at a level that will help develop a deeper relationship with a spouse is a long and very intangible one. It's an ongoing process that takes time. But it's time well spent. Again, it's something about which a parent will be able to say, "I'm glad I did." Watching an adult child fumble through a marriage, unable to communicate, to express feelings, would cause the parent to say, "I wish I had."

SUMMARY

1. One of the areas where young people are unprepared for marriage is their inability to communicate.

2. Communication is a process that needs to be "caught and taught" at home.
3. Today's parents have often become overly "project oriented" in their communication patterns with their children.
4. Parents need to take the time to be more "feelings oriented." Understanding the verbal expression of feelings is a great asset for developing a strong marriage.

QUESTIONS

1. How do you communicate with your child? Do you talk about feelings?
2. How can you set up a plan that will help your children learn to express gratitude?
3. Remorse is an important feeling in all relationships. How well do the members of your family express remorse? What steps can you take to improve that area of communication?
4. When is the best time in your family to sit and talk privately with a child about a specific feeling the child is dealing with?

Chapter Thirteen

Prepare Them to Handle Money or Money Will Handle Them

"I can't believe I'm sitting here having this discussion," Leon began. "I make more than enough money . . . in fact, more money than I ever dreamed I'd be making. But no matter how much I make, we still seem to live hand to mouth. Each year I set big financial goals and each year I reach them. But that doesn't seem to matter. It just doesn't matter what my income is. There's never enough.

"All Betty and I do is argue about how to spend it or what we can't afford to get. The more I make, the more we argue. It's ridiculous! There actually seems to be a relationship between our income and our arguments. The more I make, the more we seem to spend, and the more we argue. I'm convinced that there's no such thing as enough income."

Leon had come for help with his financial and marital woes. What pushed him to seek help was hearing his friend Tony talk in church one Sunday. Tony had said how grateful he was to be able to give a tithe and an offering. That started Leon thinking. He knew he probably made a lot more money than Tony did, yet Tony was able to tithe and give an additional offering. He seemed to be able to do a lot more with his income. How did he do it? Leon couldn't figure it out.

With that statement, Leon revealed more of himself and the conflicts going on in his marriage than he had ever been willing to share with anyone before. He'd been trained to earn a good income, but he'd never learned how to handle money. This lack of money sense was causing a great conflict in his marriage and in the rest of his life.

Leon was an attorney, accustomed to being the one in control of all conversations. But as he talked, he came to close to losing control of his emotions. He said he learned a valuable lesson from his friend that day. Tony had told him, "It's not the income that counts, it's the outgo. You seem to have no plan for your spending. Without a plan for your spending, you are set up to react to every spending opportunity that flashes before your eyes. You are also set up to do a lot of arguing with Betty.

"Start with a plan and then discipline yourself to live within the plan. Otherwise, your outgo will be in a constant race with your income, but the biggest race will be between you and Betty: Who will get to the money and spend it first?"

UNPREPARED

Once again we're looking at a very significant area of life for which our children are totally unprepared. Because they are unprepared to handle the discipline of finances, finances are handling them. They're being forced to work harder, often at jobs they really don't like, so they can keep up with the spending. They are working harder because they are not budgeting.

> *Start with a plan and then discipline yourself to live within the plan.*

How many young people got out of college with two things—a diploma and a credit card? All of a sudden their senior year, the card appeared in the mailbox. The credit card company "honored" them by saying they were "pre-approved." All they had to do was fill out a form and the card was theirs for the using. Before long they found themselves facing years of trying to get out from under their huge debt. The credit card that was meant to be a convenience became a monthly nightmare.

TWO BASIC BLESSINGS OF CONFLICT

When couples are asked what they spend the most time arguing about, most say that one of the areas of conflict that continually comes up is money. Having money to spend is meant to be a blessing to the marriage. We are blessed with the opportunity to make money for our families. God could have made us beg for our existence, but he didn't do that. God gave us the privilege of money. Blessing or burden? It is the parents' responsibility to prepare a child to be able to handle this blessing rather than bear the burden.

START THE DISCIPLINE OF FINANCES EARLY

The first step in the process of preparing a child to handle money is to have some money to handle. It's hard to learn about money if there's no money to learn with. Children should be given an allowance at an early age. They need the opportunity to make personal decisions about money. Sure, they're going to fail with their money. But childhood is the best time to fail. Money is one of those disciplines that people only seem to learn by making mistakes. It makes more sense to give a child the opportunity to learn by making mistakes with an allowance than it does to watch a young adult make dramatic mistakes with a whole year's wages. There are just too many ways for a young adult to make foolish financial decisions, mistakes that are painful for a parent to watch. It makes sense, therefore, for a child to have an opportunity to make and learn from financial mistakes.

When parents start preparing their children to be successful at the discipline of finances, there are three initial questions that have to be answered:

- How young to start an allowance?
- How much should the allowance be?
- Is the allowance compensation for anything?

It makes more sense to give a child the opportunity to learn by making mistakes with an allowance than it does to watch a young adult make dramatic mistakes with a whole year's wages.

The younger you start a child learning about money the better. Today's marketing world targets children the minute they are able to watch television or open a toy catalog. In fact, even the grocery store places certain items for toddlers at their eye level. Think about the gum, toy, and helmet machines perched at toddler level on a stand that moms with young tots must walk past as they leave the grocery store.

The younger you start a child learning about money the better.

Most children are ready to receive a weekly allowance at about four years old. The initial amount of money should be just enough to put a minimal amount of spending power, and thus decision-making power, in their lap. Until the day comes when the four- or five-year-old realizes that these coins can be exchanged for things they want in those grocery store machines, parents will probably find the money left lying around the house.

One dollar is probably a sufficient amount to start this young spender with. Once the amount has been established, an announcement needs to be made. "Billy," a mom can begin, "from now on I won't be giving you the quarters to put into those little baseball helmet machines at the grocery store. Instead, we're going to give you an allowance each week and you can use that money for anything you want to buy when we go grocery shopping."

Obviously, further definition will need to be given regarding what the child can buy with the allowance. The key here is establishing the age to begin and then the amount to give. Once these are decided, it's best for the parents to get out of the way and allow the child to make decisions. There is very little doubt about whether young children will instantly become adept at handling the outgo of money. But let them do it. On their own. Better to waste money now than when they are Leon's age. Childhood is the time to learn.

Having made the connection between the allowance and the helmet machine at the store, Billy will no longer leave his coins lying around the house. Instead he'll deposit every coin he has in the helmet machine. He learns quickly that once he's spent it all, it's time to go back to the old system. "Mom, I spent all my money and I didn't get one of those Florida Marlins helmets. That one right there." Johnny points to one that looks as if it would be the next one to fall through the slot if he only had more money to plug in. He is trying to establish a new system of "first I'll spend mine and then I'll spend yours." Don't let that happen. Just keep pushing the cart out the door of the grocery store and say, "Honey, you know I said that once you spent all your money, that would be it until next week."

SPEND IT WITH BOUNDARIES

It's important to let children develop their own spending discipline, but it's also important to let them know there are things they are not permitted to buy. When our son, Robey, was five, our arrangement was that when he had saved four dollars or more, we would go to a large local toy store. The second trip turned out to be much like the first. Robey searched the store for a toy figure he wanted and each time selected some grotesque monster that we would not permit him to buy. Then he presented his argument. "Daddy, I thought you said it was my money and I could buy anything I want as long as I have enough money. This is what I want to buy."

And I'd present my rebuttal. "There are thousands of toys in this store. Only a few of them are unacceptable for you to buy. For two trips now you have asked if you can bring these kinds of ugly monsters home. Last time I explained why you can't buy one of these. Do you remember what we talked about? You're asking the wrong question. Ask me some 'yes' questions. You keep bringing me toys I have to say no to. Bring me toys to look at that I can say yes to. Show me a 'yes' toy!"

It wasn't his fault for asking if he could buy the wrong toy. He was just testing the rules. Just because I had spelled out the spending rules on the first trip didn't mean to him that we'd have the same rules this time. He was also learning about consistency. The fault would have been mine had I changed the rule from one time to the next. These are great opportunities to teach consistent living as well as financial discipline.

There will always be things that we might be able to afford but that we should be disciplined enough not to purchase. Letting children spend their own money, within parameters, will help prepare them for that. Some parents are stumped when they find that one of their teens has purchased a music CD that had previously been termed unacceptable by the parent. "What do I do now?" a parent asked. "He has made this purchase of a horrible CD, but he paid for it with his own money."

That parent should treat the CD just as we would have treated one of those forbidden monster toys. If our son somehow had gone against the rules of our home and brought "a monster" into our home, it would have been thrown out.

"But Mom," the teen will protest, "I paid for that with my own money."

The response needs to be loving but firm. "You may purchase many things with your money. But there are some things that are unacceptable. When you choose to make those purchases and bring them into our home, they will be thrown out. Please think about this before you buy something."

In other words, "Ask me the 'yes' questions."

WARNING: GRANDPARENTS MIGHT BE HAZARDOUS TO YOUR PLAN

"But what do I do when I get this plan for teaching financial discipline all in place and my parents blow it all out of whack by giving them money?" a discouraged parent complained. "Then I feel as if we're wasting our time."

Don't for a minute think that you are going to be able to pull all grandparents into this plan. But then, that's one of the beauties of grandparents. They can supply so many of the extras. We all get bonuses every now and then, finding or receiving money that we didn't expect. Remember that the purpose of this plan is not built around how much a child receives, but that the child must learn to handle the amount received. From the parent, the child will only be receiving a specific amount of money each week. Generally speaking, this is the money the child will have to learn to "live on."

WHAT'S THE CONNECTION BETWEEN CHORES AND ALLOWANCE?

Parents often ask, "What's the connection between chores and allowance?" The response to that question is somewhat controversial. It is my opinion that children should not be paid to be a family member. In other words, I don't believe there should be any connection between chores and an allowance. All children should have chores to do (as has been previously described in this book). They should be required to do chores simply because they are a member of the family. No one pays the other members of the household for work that needs to be done. Mom doesn't get paid for cooking dinner. Dad doesn't get paid to do the dishes. No one gets paid for doing the laundry. Why would we teach a child to expect to be paid to help the family? That only fosters an attitude of "What will I get if I do that?"

Children should be required to do chores simply because they are a member of the family.

"Trevor, I need you to help me get things down from the attic this morning. We're going to bring down the Christmas tree decorations," a dad might say. A son who is used to being paid each week for doing things for the family will quite naturally respond with "How much will I get for this?" His response is not motivated so much by greed, but by training. He thinks of getting paid when he does things for the family rather than thinking that being a member of a family means that everyone pitches in to do their part.

Children should receive a weekly allowance. And they must be required to do weekly chores. The two aren't connected. But there's nothing wrong with having an extra job list that gives a child an opportunity to make a little extra money. The extra job list is a list of tasks that are beyond the scope of the child's chores. The child can get paid for doing them. Each job pays a certain amount. This is a list the child can see and decide which jobs to do in order to make extra money.

There's another advantage to this extra job list. It can be used to teach a child salesmanship and negotiation and pricing.

One Saturday, Robey wanted to earn some extra money, so I offered to pay him three dollars to wash my van. He was already washing his mother's car as one of his chores.

"Three dollars!" he complained. "That's not enough to wash your van. It should be more."

"Why should it be more?" I responded. "It only costs me three dollars to get it washed when I get it filled up with gas. I'd rather give you the money for a wash than give it to a machine."

"But Dad," he continued, trying to win me over, "that's a machine wash. A hand wash is much better than a machine wash. How about five dollars to wash your van?"

"You're right. A hand wash *can* be much better than a machine wash. I'll go to four dollars, but that's it."

I don't mind the debate. I enjoy teaching how to negotiate in a respectful manner. Salesmanship is something that will be important in the future. I also want to teach him how to work for his money. The weekly allowance is set and reset at the beginning of each school year. If he wants more money, he has to be willing to find extra work to earn it.

TAKE ADVANTAGE OF TEACHING OPPORTUNITIES

Vacations can be a whining nightmare for parents. "Can I have that?" "Will you buy me that?" "Why can't I have that?" Sometimes it seems like children think vacations are a time when parents have unending wealth in their pockets. A vacation can be a time of constant arguing (hardly a vacation), or it can be a great opportunity for training. The responsibility for what the children spend needs to be put on their shoulders rather than on the adults.

Each year on vacation, we have made an arrangement with our children that we will match whatever money they have saved by the day before we leave for vacation. This is something that they know and can choose to save toward. Robey was seven the first year we did this. The day before we were to leave for the mountains of North Carolina, the children each came to show me what they had saved. Robey had saved twenty-six dollars. So there he was at seven with fifty-two dollars in a cowboy wallet that was half hanging out of his pocket as we visited various places in the mountains.

I wanted to say to him, "Why don't you let me hold that wallet for you so you don't lose it?" But part of becoming financially responsible is to learn to keep track of where your wallet is. Everybody loses their wallet once in life, and then they become more careful. This time, he didn't lose his wallet. That came a couple years later.

The first day we went into the town near where we were staying, Robey was primed. He had all this money. We walked into the first store and it just happened to be a store that had a lot of things he wanted, so he started stocking up. He bought a rubber knife, a spear, a plastic bow and arrow, and a battery-powered water gun. (All the moms reading this section are now shocked and wondering what kind of a child we're raising, buying all those weapons! Maybe the answer lies in the fact that his dad went back in the store and bought the same battery-powered water gun for himself! It was great!)

As Robey was gathering his loot, his sage sister tried to stop him. "This is just the first day of vacation. If you spend all your money now, you won't have any more for the rest of the two weeks. And Daddy's not going to give you any more." Being older and more experienced, she understood the system. Robey still had to learn.

"I don't care," was his response. "This is all I want. I won't need to get anything else."

Even when we tried to talk to him about the fact that the plastic bow and arrow weren't going to make it through the day, he still wouldn't listen. This was an opportunity to teach a great lesson. Difficult as it was, we all got out of the way and let him make his own decisions. And he did. Robey spent almost all of his money that first morning. He had less than two dollars left when he was done. But he was ecstatic as he walked out of the store with an armload of plastic weapons!

Most mornings after that were difficult for Robey. We would go back to town and I'd get my traditional cup of coffee and a newspaper and sit on a bench. The ladies in our family would spend a few hours shopping. Robey would sit by me sadly sipping his soda. (Each day I'd buy each of the children a soda or an ice cream, but that was it.)

"This isn't any fun for me," he announced one day. "I don't have any money to spend." The temptation was great. I could have been a real hero that day by slipping him a few bucks and chalking his failure up to inexperience. But I didn't. This was a lesson he needed to learn. It was tough on both of us.

Financial discipline is a lesson every child needs to learn. Rather than be a hero when they're seven, be a hero for a lifetime. Stick with the plan so that later on in life you'll be able to say, "I'm glad I did," rather than "I wish I had."

GRADUATE THE PLAN

As children grow older, more and more financial decisions need to be put into their hands. Better to have them make financial mistakes while they're still home, rather than when they are sitting a thousand miles away in a college dormitory or an apartment. Childhood is the time to practice, while they're still home and parents can help them figure things out.

Before your teen leaves home, make sure that he or she has spent a period of time being totally responsible for a budget.

Many parents postpone turning financial decisions over to a teen until the day the child is dropped off on that college campus or at the door of their first apartment. Then, for the first time, that young person becomes responsible for a checkbook and a financial system. No wonder they call home only to say, "Send money!" They've had no practice in managing money except to spend it. And they're still spending, with no idea how to balance income and outgo. No wonder Leon and his wife were arguing about their different spending habits. That was the only habit they had been taught.

Before your teen leaves home, make sure that he or she has spent a period of time being totally responsible for a budget. Ideally, this can take place at the start of the junior year of high school. This is a time when a budget can be set up and reviewed for all the teen's needs, from cosmetics to clothes to the after-church fast-food meals with the youth group. Once the monthly needs of the teen have been evaluated, including things such as contact lens cleaner that Mom usually purchases at the store, then it's time for the teen to live within a budget.

BUDGET ENVELOPES

One plan that has worked in many homes is an envelope system. The teen sets up six or seven envelopes labeled for the week-to-week needs. One envelope can be for church activities, one for cosmetics and toiletries, one for friends and family members' birthdays gifts, one for clothes, and one for tithe. Each week, or twice a month, a specific amount of money can be given to the teen to be placed in each envelope. This is enough money to meet the needs. If the teen wants to purchase a new outfit, then the clothing envelope will have to go untouched for a period of time to build up enough money in that envelope to make the purchase. Learning to save for something you want is a necessary part of handling money in the adult world.

It matters not that a child comes from a wealthy family, where money is plentiful. A teen will still need to learn how to live within a budget. This is all part of financial discipline. The teen needs the opportunity to live through the tough financial decisions of holding off spending in one area in order to be able to purchase something else. One father using this plan commented, "One of my daughter's envelopes was for her lunches. It initially broke my heart to hear that she was skipping some of her lunches at school in order to save up money for a dress she wanted. Then after I thought about it, I realized that that is exactly what I have done from time to time, skipped something I wanted for something else I wanted even more. It's a taste of the real world."

From time to time, parents can review the envelopes with the teen to see how things are going. If it's not working, back off for a period of time. That's the beauty of training teens while they're still living at home. But don't be afraid to return to this system before too long. This is a lesson that a child will have to learn before he or she leaves home. If not, problems with money will plague them much of their adult life.

The envelope system gives teens an opportunity to practice the freedom of making their own financial decisions. Should they buy this item now or wait and buy it when it's on sale? It was amazing how the envelope system changed our daughter's view of spending concerning a simple item like shampoo. In tenth grade, when Mom was purchasing shampoo with grocery money, Torrey had to have the latest shampoo that was being advertised on television. In eleventh grade, when she was using her money to purchase shampoo, we began seeing huge budget bottles of generic shampoo in her bathroom. The latest, expensive shampoos were worth *our* money to her, but they were no longer worth her own money.

Put in a plan, and get out of the way. Let them practice while you are there to observe. It's too late if you've waited until they're a thousand miles away from home. Then you can't observe or advise or help. You can only bail them out or watch them drown.

WHAT? A CREDIT CARD?

At some point while children are still living at home, parents need to let teens practice using a credit card. Now, after you've picked yourself up off the floor, think about it. It's the credit card that gets many adults into trouble. It's the plastic that plagues many marriages. But it's not the credit card that causes all these problems; credit cards are a convenience. The problem comes from inexperience in the use of a credit card. Before we know it, that convenience becomes a condemnation in our lives. That's why it's absolutely mandatory for a teen to practice with a credit card before leaving home.

This is a great opportunity for the senior year of high school. A credit card established with the lowest limit your local back will allow is the way to begin. It's important to teach a teen that the purpose of this card is only for financial convenience. The entire balance of the card will need to be paid out of the envelopes each and every month. The month the bill comes in and the balance can't be paid from the envelopes, the card is taken away by the parent, to be returned only when the balance is paid in full.

Doesn't that make much more sense than giving a teen a credit card for the first time as you're saying those emotional good-byes on the dormitory steps? All too often that emotion turns to anger and frustration when bills that are overdue and can't be paid arrive in the mail. The teen then places frantic, tearful calls to Mom and Dad. Collect calls. That scenario is almost guaranteed when parents fail to supply the hands-on instruction before their child leaves home.

WHAT ABOUT TEACHING THEM TO SAVE?

Many financial experts encourage parents to teach their children to save money. In order to get them to save some money, however, parents might have to force children to put part of their money in some sort of savings account. But there's a better way to teach a child to save. When parents have in place a learning plan that teaches the children that they are responsible for their purchases, most teens will eventually become aware of the fact that they will never be able to purchase anything that costs more than their weekly allowance unless they find a way to accumulate a lump sum. The child now becomes responsible for saving money, not just spending it.

When Robey was eleven, he came to me two weeks before we were to leave on vacation and asked if he could be given his matching vacation money before we were to leave for the mountains. "Why do you want it so early?" I said.

His answer amazed me. "Because I've been able to save $148 this year. When you give me the matching funds I'll have almost $300. I want to take my money and put it in the bank, and I'll take the matching funds to spend on vacation."

He'd learned the lesson too well! He had learned to save. And I learned two lessons. The first was that, placed in a structured financial plan, my children eventually learned to save on their own, and that's the best way to learn. Making their own decisions, they have a much stronger motivation to save. The second lesson I learned was to put a cap of $100 on what I will match!

WHAT ABOUT TITHING?

One of the most difficult lessons for me to learn was the obedience of giving back to God. We all have an innate selfishness that makes it difficult to give anything away. This is a lesson that comes much easier when it is taught to the child as an automatic part of the financial plan. There are many wives who feel torn because they want to give ten percent to their church, but their husbands do not. Most of the time the husband's inability to trust God with his finances is due to a lack of training.

When starting your five-year-old with a dollar allowance, give it in dimes. At the same time, have your church send your child a set of offering envelopes. By doing this, the child will learn much more than tithing. The child will learn not to be greedy. Money can be something that you use or it can be a consuming item that uses you. You either own it to do with as you please, or it seems to own you and you can't let go of it. Greed is a powerful illness. Teaching children to tithe is an opportunity to teach obedience as well as generosity. It's a lesson that will bless their lives.

LET GO

It's extremely important to raise children in such a way that they will be able to become financially responsible adults. The importance of letting go cannot be overstated. Both young children and teens must have the opportunity to be able to make financial decisions. This is one area where we can allow them to fail. The results of financial failure are correctable. Let go and let them make their own mistakes.

One spring Robey was killing time by looking through a men's clothing catalog that had just come in the mail. He discovered a very in-vogue pair of name-brand sandals that were on sale. My ordinarily frugal son decided that he *had* to have the sandals. I looked at what he wanted and saw sandals that looked like a used tire tread with a colorful guitar strap to go over the foot. All for a mere fifty-eight dollars!

"Robey," I protested, "these sandals seem awfully expensive."

"Oh, no, Dad," he insisted. "These are the in things. Everybody has them, and this is what they cost."

After asking him if he wouldn't rather first take a look in some of the local stores to see if he could get a better deal, he responded with, "No, Dad. This is what I want. If I give you the money and the shipping charges, will you order them for me on your credit card?" It was his money, so against my better judgment, I ordered the sandals.

Later on that summer we were at a family reunion and Robey's cousins arrived. The first one out of the van was his cousin Erin. She's a year older and very cool! Robey and I went out to greet them and Robey immediately noticed that Erin had on the same sandals. "Look, Dad," he said very triumphantly. "Erin has the same sandals."

"These aren't the expensive kind," Erin said. "These are clones."

I couldn't help myself. "Erin, how much did those sandals cost?"

She paid eleven dollars. Isn't God good to give us those teaching moments?

Leave them alone and let them learn. Peer pressure will cause them to make a lot of their financial decisions. I'd rather have them spend too much money on a pair of sandals as a child than buy a sports car they can't afford as an adult. Set up a system that will let them learn.

SUMMARY

1. The number-one area for marital conflict today is finances. We must not send our children into adulthood without any financial training.
2. Put a plan in place early in your child's life that will help your child practice handling money.
3. Before a teen leaves home, he or she must have had the opportunity to practice being responsible for all their expenses.
4. Before a teen leaves home, he or she must have had experience being responsible for a credit card.

QUESTIONS

1. Look at the financial plan that you are using to train your child. Is it adequate?
2. Decide ahead of time what items your child is not permitted to purchase. Then get out of the way and let them work on their spending.
3. Set an age and an amount of money to start giving your child an allowance.
4. For your teens, spend time enumerating all their day-to-day expenses. Help your teens set up an envelope system that puts the decisions for all these purchases in their hands.

Chapter Fourteen

—◦—

Sex Is Not a Four-Letter Word

I really want to buy this book," a woman said to us as she stood in front of our book tables. Rosemary and I were presenting a marriage seminar at her church, and she was looking at a copy of our book *Great Sexpectations*. "I really want to buy it," she said again, "but I know he won't read it with me. Ronny refuses to talk about our sex life. We've been married for twenty-two years and this is an area that needs lots of help, but it's also an area that we just can't discuss. It's very frustrating for both of us. I know we're missing out, and it's all because we don't talk to each other."

One husband sat in my office and said, "This really makes me mad. Everything you're telling me about my wife's sexual needs is brand-new information to me. How could I be so uninformed? Why is it so difficult for me to even talk with her about this? I get so uncomfortable when we talk about sex, and because of that I feel like we're missing out on a lot!"

—◦—

The different points of view concerning the sexual relationship become a major conflict when one of the spouses refuses to discuss these differences.

—◦—

This man's problem was not at all unusual. Sex is one of the primary areas of conflict in the marriage. It is a conflict caused by silence. Frustration due to ignorance. There is a total lack of understanding about the differing points of view each spouse has. The needs and desires of the husband are totally different and often opposed to the needs and desires of the wife. But that in and of itself is not the real problem. The different points of view concerning the sexual relationship become a major conflict when one of the spouses refuses to discuss these differences. The silence is the cause of the conflict.

Had this man's parents opened the doors of communication about his sexuality, he would have at least been able to talk to his wife. Communication about sex in marriage is half the battle. His parents could have gotten him halfway there.

WHY THE SILENCE?

The topic of sexuality is a very prevalent one in our society today. It's exploited in advertising, on television, and in conversation. The topic of sex might be used to draw people's attention to things like billboards, but the actual nuances of a good sexual relationship are rarely, if ever, taught. No one can teach the specific issues of a sexual relationship better than one's own spouse. Who knows better about their sexual needs than that person?

The culture, especially the male half, has become sexually aroused but not sexually educated.

The very fact that there is so much talk about the physical nature of sex has played a part in making it difficult to talk about it in the intimate setting of the marriage. It can make the typical uninformed person feel almost childish to admit that she, or even more likely he, doesn't really understand the other spouse sexually.

"I know we should have come in to seek help sooner." A husband explained his discomfort. "But this is so hard. It's so hard for me to say that I don't know what to do for her sexually. I somehow feel less masculine saying that. It's a hard discussion. In fact, it's even hard for me to use those words you're using." He was referring to words that describe the sexual anatomy, and he had an even more difficult time with words that describe the act of sex, such as *orgasm* or *erection*. Never having used these words before, he had a difficult time using them now, especially when talking to his wife.

We have raised two generations that have become sexually aroused by the sensuality of our culture. Sex is such a powerful tool on television, billboards, and so forth. The culture, especially the male half, has become sexually aroused but not sexually educated. He is stimulated, but not accustomed to talking about or listening to a discussion about sex with his spouse. That can be very frustrating for both husband and wife. And, as I said, this frustration can escalate into major conflicts. These conflicts can be alleviated, to some extent, by proper training during childhood.

Many parents believe that the primary reason to talk to their children and teens about sex, is to help them stay pure before marriage. To help them wait. That is certainly one reason, but not the primary reason. The most important reason to open the door of communication about sex is to help children and teens develop a comfort level when it comes to sexual discussions. Opening this door by an ongoing discussion and education at home helps to make it possible for children to ask questions. If this is a topic that is discussed openly and freely, the child and teen will feel more comfortable discussing this very important topic—both as a child and later as an adult. Most importantly, when married, your child will not feel squeamish talking about sex with a spouse.

> *The most important reason to open the door of communication about sex is to help children and teens develop a comfort level when it comes to sexual discussions.*

"Buy that book! Why would I buy that book?" another wife lamented while once again holding up a copy of *Great Sexpectations*.

"Buy it so you two can read it together," I answered her.

"Look!" this wife said, showing more and more frustration as the conversation continued. "For years I've tried to get him to talk to me about our sexual relationship. I've tried to talk. I've cut out articles. I've even tried to read paragraphs to him. He just doesn't want to talk about it. One time, when I put a magazine opened to an article titled *Understanding Your Wife's Sexual Needs* on his bedside table, and he just used it for an iced tea coaster. When I couldn't stand it anymore, I asked him if he was going to read the article and all he said was, 'If you have a sexual problem, you read it. I don't need any help!'"

I had contact with that particular couple for a while. He obviously did have a sexual problem, as his wife went on to have an affair with another man in their neighborhood. Only when he was broken and suffering did he open up and admit to needing to learn more about her.

Sex is a very powerful force in our culture. But simply displaying body parts on billboards or showing two people groping each other in a movie does not present an accurate view or a complete education of sex and what it means in a marriage relationship. Because our picture of what sex is and what it involves is often based solely on what our culture presents, we become embarrassed when we are trapped into thinking that we're the only adults who don't understand the needs of the opposite sex.

ANATOMY

Many couples who go for counseling have to first overcome the difficulty of using the right words when it comes to sex. Had they been trained from the beginning by parents who insisted on using the right anatomical names for the parts of the body, this first obstacle would have been overcome. Start your children on their journey to sexual understanding by teaching them the correct parts of the body, using the proper anatomical names.

We don't use a nickname when teaching the children the proper name for the elbow. Why do we use nicknames when labeling the sexual anatomy? Often we impose our own sexual discomfort or hang-ups when we begin teaching children about their sexuality.

A penis is a penis, and we need to label it as such for children. No doubt, just as soon as we teach them these correct labels, we're going to hear them shout the correct labels down the halls of the church nursery! It's worth our embarrassment.

This lesson in anatomy should begin when they are still young enough to ask questions. Three years old is when they are pointing to themselves and asking, "What's this, Daddy?" It makes sense that we should be teaching anatomy when our children are at that age.

For young children who have the privilege of being in homes where Mom becomes pregnant, there's the opportunity to answer the question, "How will he get out of your tummy, Mommy?" That's the time to explain to the child that the baby will come out into the world through the opening in Mommy's vagina "just like you did, honey."

The reason to start children's sexual education is to help them become comfortable with the use of the correct language. If they grow up in a home where the proper words for the sexual anatomy are used and

If they grow up in a home where the proper words for the sexual anatomy are used and used frequently enough to make a child feel comfortable both using them and hearing them, marriage discussions will be much easier.

used frequently enough to make a child feel comfortable both using them and hearing them, marriage discussions will be much easier. That's one hurdle that will already be overcome. Many men might be comfortable using street terms for sex but find it difficult to use the proper terms. Early childhood home life can play a great part in easing that discomfort. Use the right words.

BIOLOGY

The next logical step after helping a child through the basic anatomy is the biology of procreation and birth. Using the proper anatomical terms might be difficult for many parents, but the teaching of the biology of the union of the egg and sperm is far more difficult.

"Is this really necessary?" one parent asked. "Why do we have to teach them how babies are made?"

It's not a matter of telling the child how babies are made. It's creating an open door to an ongoing discussion about the biology of sexuality. Open and easy, so that children can ask questions as they grow up in the home. Making it easier for them to be able to hear the important information about their sexuality so that they can come to the parent to ask questions, rather than keep their ear to the streets, hoping they'll pick up this much sought after information from the jokes they hear at school.

Even more significant is the fact that they need to feel comfortable discussing this information as a child and teen, so that they can feel comfortable discussing it with their spouse. How will they learn about the sexuality of their spouse if they can't discuss it with their spouse? This will be a difficult topic for them as adults if it's a taboo topic when they're children and teens. This subject is not only informational for the children, but it's also a practice time of discussions that will impact their comfort zones when they are married. As difficult as these discussions might be for some parents, they will certainly impact the child's future marriage discussions. But these discussions are probably only difficult for the parents who never had these discussions when they were children. It's time to break the cycle and remove any barriers in the way of a fulfilled sexual relationship in the child's future marriage.

The teaching of the biological facts usually progresses as the questions are asked. "Mommy, where do babies come from?" is a great lead in. If by seven or eight, a child hasn't yet asked those questions, it's time to begin the instruction and conversation. This conversation can be enhanced by using some of the great materials that are now available.

One of the classic books to help parents is Larry Christiansen's, *The Wonderful Way Babies Are Made*. This is a book to be read with the child. Parents should not purchase the book and give it to the child. Christiansen's book, read cover to cover at one sitting and then repeatedly over a period of time, will open the doors of communication between parent and child. It will become a more comfortable topic of discussion because the book has already broken the "word barrier."

Gone are the days when Mom should take the girls and read with them while Dad takes the boys to read the book about sex with them. Reading the book aloud can be a great mother, father, and child experience. When parents and child sit together and one parent reads out loud, it gives a child an opportunity to choose which parent he wants to ask questions to at a later time.

After reading Christiansen's book every couple of months in the evenings in our home, the door was opened. Finally, while being tucked into bed, one of our children began to ask questions. It became obvious by the question that the sexual picture was pulling together for this child. We had been reading for quite some time, but when we asked after each reading if anyone had any questions, there was always dead silence. Then months later, in the privacy of the bedroom, the questions began to flow. The door of two-way discussion was finally beginning to open. To keep those doors open, however, it was important not to answer the question in a way that goes way beyond what the child is ready to hear. Let the child's question be the guide to what is discussed. Give specific answers. If a parent jumps ahead too far, the child might be hesitant to ask questions again in the future.

> *Gone are the days when Mom should take the girls and read with them while Dad takes the boys to read the book about sex with them.*

PRE-TEENS

As young people enter those pre-teen years, where they are so aware of their emerging bodies, there are new materials for the family to graduate to. Once again, please hear the phrase, "the family." These are not materials to hand to a pre-teen, hoping they will listen to them. These are materials to be read or listened to with a parent. Remember to think ahead. The purpose of teaching in this way is not only to give information but to also give opportunity to practice communication on this topic and to make it easier for the child to eventually discuss sexual issues with a spouse.

One of the great materials available is James Dobson's tape series, *Preparing for Adolescence*. This tape album is ideal for parent and teen to listen to while driving in the car. The tapes will help open the door for difficult discussions on topics such as masturbation. Let the tapes do the hard work of bringing the topics up. Then the parent can stop a tape at any time for discussion or questions.

The pre-teen years are times of great sexual curiosity. It's a time to make the answers available. It's also a time that a parent needs to be aware of some of the other areas of sexual information input the young person is getting. Television programs that target the pre-teen are often very sexually provocative. It's also amazing how many pre-teens get much of their information from afternoon soap operas. Certainly not the bastion of responsible sexuality and mature abstinence for anyone to be absorbing, let alone a young person.

There are many great magazines that are available for pre-teens from organizations such as Focus on the Family, Campus Crusade, and the Fellowship of Christian Athletes. One of the best periodicals is *Campus Life* magazine. There are also many damaging magazines. Damaging, because some magazines seem to encourage teenage sexual experimentation by the provocative stories and columns. Read the materials your pre-teen is reading so that you can help point them in the right direction.

PURITY

The step that will permeate all sex education at home will be the lesson of purity. This lesson will be most significant during the early teenage years, however. Once again, I will not belabor an area that is covered most beautifully in many other books. Materials from Josh McDowell, such as the Why Wait series or the book *Right From Wrong* are both excellent opportunities for parent and child to study together. These materials offer a young person so much more than information. They open the door for parent and child to discuss purity as related to issues and decisions that the youth of today are facing.

Many of these materials can even be used by parent and youth for devotions. This is the time when a young person can begin to understand why God has established his plan for their sexuality—not to be a killjoy, but to help facilitate marital joy.

THE OLDER TEEN

The greatest thing a parent can do for the older teen is demonstrate a romantic marriage. Our example is so important. Teens need to know that Mom and Dad require time alone for intimacy. Explaining the exact nature of that intimacy is not necessary. Just the fact that they see us set aside the time to be alone speaks volumes. Again, how will they know to do this in their own marriages if they don't see it demonstrated at home when they are young?

The greatest thing a parent can do for the older teen is demonstrate a romantic marriage.

Purity and the reason for purity continue to be key areas of discussion during these years. There has never been a more difficult time in history for a teen to remain sexually pure. Up until recent history, a child entered puberty at eleven or twelve years old and then got married at fourteen or fifteen. In many societies, such as the Jewish culture, children were considered adults at thirteen. This left a teen only three or four years to deal with his or her sexuality. And they dealt with this sexuality in a culture that worked at protecting them from provocative sexual information and stimulation.

Today's culture is very different. Not only is today's youth bombarded by a sexually provocative society, they also enter puberty at eleven or twelve and often do not marry until they are in their early to mid twenties. That's more than a decade of living in a society that uses sexuality flippantly as an advertising tool. Also, the culture no longer takes a stand on sexual purity as a moral goal. Sex before marriage is a given. In fact, we are in a culture that increasingly confuses its youth about even which gender to be sexually active with.

Parents must stay in the training mode with their teens as they sort through the sexual jungle. The goal is purity until marriage. For quite some time our culture has tried to make parents believe that that was an unattainable goal. Now, as many youths in America are taking a stand for abstinence, parents need to help them. The lessons and decisions must be taught and decided upon long before a date. Sitting in a car or an empty house is not the time a teen should be thinking through the boundaries of sexual activity. These decisions must be discussed and decided upon long before the player hits the field.

THE GREATEST SEXUAL GIFT TO THE MARRIAGE

The reason for sexual purity is not to avoid pregnancy or disease. The reason is because it is God's prescription for people who are unmarried. It's God's plan that a man and a woman give each other their pure bodies as the ultimate wedding gift. It's God plan, and once again his plan has been backed up by research. Those who remain sexually pure prior to marriage stand a better chance of a fulfilling marriage relationship than those who don't. It is the greatest gift for a young person to be able to present at the wedding. And it is the parents' role to help facilitate the giving of that gift.

One way to help stamp this commitment in a young person's heart is to use the "Letter To Your Spouse" concept. A parent and a teen can decide to spend time together discussing the discipline and maturity of abstinence. That day should end with the youth writing a letter to their yet unmet spouse. The letter should be about their commitment to their future spouse to be pure: "I've not yet met you, but I've already made a commitment to you and to God that I will give myself only to you on our wedding night. This is my letter of commitment that I have written this day, (date) and I will hand it to you on our wedding night." This letter can include more and should be stored in a safe place so that the young person can be able to review it from time to time as well as retrieve it for the wedding.

Our job as parents is to help raise our children to be prepared for the marriage process. We are to raise them to be marriageable. One of the greatest areas of marital strife is the sexual relationship. It stands to reason that it must be a parent's responsibility to attempt to prepare the child, as much as possible, to have the resources and ability to wade through these potential difficulties.

SUMMARY

1. One of the greatest areas of conflict in the marriage relationship is the sexual area. It's not the actual act of sex that causes the conflict as much as it is the inability of many couples to talk about their sexual relationship.
2. This difficulty could be alleviated if parents spent time talking and teaching their children about sex.
3. When parents teach their children, the child and young people can then find a time when they are comfortable asking questions.
4. The process of teaching children about sex starts with anatomy, followed by biology, and then purity.

QUESTIONS

1. When is the best time for you to purchase and begin reading a book about sex with your children?
2. Is there a block of time in your family life when your children or teens can ask you questions about the readings that you have done together?
3. What ongoing method of dialogue are you using to help your teen understand God's plan for their sexuality?
4. How do you think your teen would rate your marriage, as far as the intimacy is concerned. Are you an endorsement of an exciting marriage?

RESOURCES

Christiansen, Larry; *The Wonderful Way Babies Are Made*
Dobson, James; *Preparing For Adolescence*
McDowell, Josh; *Why Wait*
McDowell, Josh; *Right From Wrong*

PART 4

Teaching the Decision-Making Template

Chapter Fifteen

Raise the Standard

Several years before the writing of this book, a man was sitting in my office about to make a very critical decision in his life. He had been married for over a decade, but he had allowed himself to develop an interest in another woman. He was having what could be called an emotional affair with a woman who was not his wife. This man, whom we will call Phil, was about to leave his wife in order to pursue this new relationship.

"Phil, we can talk about this thing for hours," I finally said to him, "but I want to ask you what you think is the *right* thing to do here." He looked at me and responded, "What's right? I know what you mean, but how could this be wrong? Part of me says leaving my wife is not the right thing to do, but being with this other person feels so good. How could it be wrong if it feels so good?" Ruled by feelings, Phil went on to leave his wife. Feelings had overtaken all reason in his life. He was responding to feelings rather than to a philosophy of life that put a standard before him and offered direction when life's decisions got momentarily blurred by feelings. He *felt* like walking away from his commitment to his marriage because of these new emotions he was experiencing. He wanted to see what life would *feel* like with this other person. His standard for life was *feelings*. His philosophy of life was to feed the appetites of his *feelings*.

Phil left his wife to be with that other person, and it wasn't until two years later that I once again encountered this broken man. He came up to me after a talk I had just finished and asked if we could have a cup of coffee together. There, over coffee, he summed up his mistake. "How could I have been so stupid to throw away my marriage? All for the momentary pleasure of another relationship."

He had no measuring stick to help him make the difficult decisions of life. No standard to help him through uncharted territory. No decision-making template to help him respond to the lifestyle he was seeing lived out by many coworkers. He hadn't been taught how to live by a philosophy of life that hinged on a higher standard than feelings. Either we are taught to live by standards, or we are taught to flap with the breeze of selfish feelings. If we are taught to live only for self, we are caught in a very shallow standard. Self gets satisfied by the good feelings of the moment. But those feelings will leave us flat and change direction when the object of our feelings no longer feels good. Feelings are like a drug. They're addicting. They are also like a flag in the wind. A flag that constantly changes direction according to the direction of the moment. This flag should sometimes be seen as a red flag, saying, "Change your direction!"

BUT FEELINGS DO REALLY HAPPEN

Our feelings are an undeniable reality and certainly not something we can ignore. In fact, feelings are a valuable part of our lives. But we have to learn decide what to do with our feelings. Either we acknowledge our feelings and keep them under our control, or we follow the flow of our culture and allow our feelings to take the lead in our decision making. Many in our culture live by the motto "If it feels good, do it. After all, you have the right." We need to help our children learn to live by the creed "If it feels good . . . first check it. Check to see if it's the *right thing to do*."

> *Either we acknowledge our feelings and keep them under our control, or we follow the flow of our culture and allow our feelings to take the lead in our decision making.*

WHOSE STANDARD?

By what standard do you determine right? Too many people today live by the standard that it's okay to do something, even if it's wrong, as long as you don't get caught. Wrong is determined by whether or not you will get caught with your hand in the middle of it. Unfortunately, getting caught doesn't even hold our culture back anymore. We've even developed a philosophy to deal with getting caught. We are now teaching the next generation that there are times that it's okay to get caught, just as long as you can justify your inappropriate behavior. You have in some way been a victim and shouldn't be held accountable. It's not really your fault. Something in your past or current surroundings leads you to do the unacceptable behavior, thus making it acceptable.

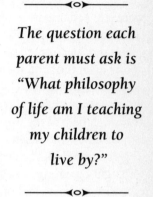

The question each parent must ask is "What philosophy of life am I teaching my children to live by?"

Society as a whole will probably spend many generations trying to correct that dilemma. Each parent must teach that "it's not my fault" is still unacceptable. By correctly teaching our children, we can personally have an impact on tomorrow. The question each parent must ask is "What philosophy of life am I teaching my children to live by?"

WE ARE TEACHING A PHILOSOPHY OF LIFE TO OUR CHILDREN

Brent Sr. was taking his son for a very significant ride in the car. Young Brent had had a problem in school that day and it was time for one of those father-and-son talks. Brent Jr. got caught breaking a rule and then tried to lie his way out of it. Brent's wife was devastated by the whole incident and suggested that he take his son for a ride and have a talk about the importance of integrity.

"Son, I know you think that the rule you broke is a stupid rule, but that's not the point. Just because you think the rule is not important doesn't give you the right to decide to break it. Rules are made for a reason. It might be our job to find ways to discuss the rules if we think they're wrong, but it's also our responsibility to obey them until they're changed."

Then just as father and son were turning off the road they were on and entering the interstate, as a matter of habit, Brent Sr. turned to his son and said what he always said when they entered the highway: "Flip on the radar detector, will you, son?"

No sooner was it out of his mouth, than this dad realized how sad his example was. The words "Rules are made to be followed" were still echoing in the car, and here he was asking his son to turn on a device that electronically helped them break the traffic rules. Using this electronic rule breaker had become such a habit that he hadn't even thought about it. Without thinking about the ramifications of it, Brent had begun to use the radar detector several years prior to this father/son teaching time. It was fun and made him feel as though he had the upper hand and was outsmarting the police. It helped him avoid tickets. It helped him break the rules without getting caught. He had never really thought about whether using one was right or wrong, let alone what he was teaching his son. "Everyone" else he knew had one, why not him?

Why not? Because it's wrong to break the rules just because you don't agree with them. Once again, it all stems back to philosophy of life. Are we teaching one philosophy of life and then living out a different philosophy of life? Are we living a philosophy of life that will bless the lives of our children when they become adults? One that will help them remember how we made our decisions, so they can draw from our examples? Or are we cursing them by leaving them without any absolutes other than "if it feels good it must be okay to do or have what you want"?

EVERY CHILD WILL LEAVE HOME HAVING SEEN A PHILOSOPHY OF LIFE

Philosophy of life offers each of us direction when we need to make decisions. When faced with a new situation, perhaps in a new environment, my philosophy of life is all I have to help me decide whether or not this action is acceptable. Without a solid standard to fall back on, I'm prone to follow the pressure of the crowd that is around me or my feelings of the moment.

"What a bunch of baloney," one man exclaimed after a seminar. "I don't have this mystical philosophy of life. Who does? Everybody, as you say, doesn't operate with a philosophy of life!"

Quite the contrary. Everyone does have a personal philosophy that they live by, but many people don't realize it. Some people live by feelings. Some people live by going after position. They spend the days talking and dreaming about the fact that if they could just get that job or promotion, or if they could just live in that house or part of the country, then they'd be truly happy. They believe they will finally find contentment when they get something or live somewhere. Their philosophy of life is do what it takes to make that happen. Whether they would actually claim this as their philosophy of life or even understand that it is, is immaterial. The fact that this is the criteria they use to make their decisions makes it the philosophy of life they live by. Consciously chosen by them or not, it's still their ruling philosophy of life.

When faced with a new situation, perhaps in a new environment, my philosophy of life is all I have to help me decide whether or not this action is acceptable.

As children grow up in their homes listening to their parents talking about whatever they are in pursuit of, they become aware that this is the goal: "Getting these things will make my parents happy. This is what we're here to do." The chief end of man is the pursuit of things. In fact, our decisions will wrap around these pursuits.

At first glance this sounds overstated. But our children are growing up watching us and learning the way we make decisions. They are watching the standards we set for ourselves. The way we make decisions, coupled with the way their peers make decisions, will help to form the basis for the template they will use to make their own decisions about life's opportunities. This will help to form the construct for their philosophy of life.

Nothing will impact tomorrow in a child's or adult's life as much as this one area of training. Being employable is very important, but

━━━◄○►━━━

The way we make decisions, coupled with the way our children's peers make decisions, will help to form the basis for the template our kids will use to make their own decisions about life's opportunities.

━━━◄○►━━━

a person's philosophy of life will govern many decisions a person makes while employed or away on business trips. It will even affect which places of employment he or she will choose. Being marriageable is crucial. But a spouse's philosophy of life will be the key factor governing fidelity in that marriage. Staying faithful to a marriage should not be contingent on whether or not my spouse is meeting my needs (making me feel good). No other person can meet my needs. Philosophy of life will determine the direction of a marriage. Especially during the difficult times every marriage must endure.

Life's most significant institutions—employment and family—are both governed by one's philosophy of life. If acquisition is what governs my life, I'll take any promotion or make any move to fulfill my desires to acquire. In fact, I'll do anything to get that promotion so I can make that acquisition. If feeling good rules my life, then there is no telling what I'll do. After all, anything's okay as long as I don't get caught.

When all is said and done in this life, can a person sit down and say to himself, "the philosophy of life I used to make my decisions, has permitted me to say I'm glad I did the things I did"? Or, as someone has said, will he have to say he spent a lifetime climbing the ladder of success only to find it leaning up against the wrong wall? "I wish I had . . ."

WHAT PHILOSOPHY OF LIFE DO I WANT TO TEACH?

It's always amazing to see what happens when many young couples have their first child. For many, the birth of the child marks the point at which they start thinking about going back to church. Their child, they think, needs some kind of religious education. Why? When one new couple in church was asked that question they responded with "because I want my child to grow up learning right from wrong." They wanted church in their lives so that the child could learn a philosophy of life that contained absolutes.

Church is an important ingredient, but church alone will not give a child a philosophy of life to live by. Church will give a child a location to go to hear about a way of life that is often different from that of home or peers. Parents are the ones who need to do the teaching. Parents are the ones who need to set the example. Parents are the ones who need to illustrate for the child an actual philosophy of life that is worthy of spending a lifetime using as a template for decision making. Going to church or dropping the children off at a church won't make the children strong Christians any more than standing in the garage one hour a week will turn my children into a car. It's not where we go that teaches these all important lessons of life. It's how we live.

> *Going to church or dropping the children off at a church won't make the children strong Christians any more than standing in the garage one hour a week will turn my children into a car.*

YES, BUT . . .

"That's great, but my husband . . ." I can almost hear a reader saying right now. There are no "yes, buts" where philosophy of life is concerned. As you read this portion of the book, don't waste any energy thinking about the inconsistencies in a spouse's life. "Oh, if I could only get my husband to just read this part. Maybe if I left it opened at this part, he'd pick it up." No one is responsible for a spouse or an ex-spouse. God will only hold me personally responsible for my own personal efforts. My personal philosophy of life is the issue here, not someone else's.

Any philosophy of life other than a faith in God is leaving a child far short of what he or she deserves. The manufacturer or creator of humankind and of our children personally has a much better idea of how to live this life than any momentary cultural whim. Why, when it comes to training our children, do we as parents so quickly respond to the whims of our culture, rather than the time-tested instructions of our God? Faith is more than going to church. It's living a life that would lead my child to follow Jesus Christ.

THE OWNER'S MANUAL

Some time ago I bought a new barbecue grill. One of the things that drew me toward that grill was the sign that said "easily assembled." I like that. Once the grill was out of the box and sitting on the floor of my garage, I took a momentary glance at the instruction book and then I began to put it together ... without reading any further. After all, I knew I didn't really need the directions. I'm an intelligent human being. (Actually, an intelligent human being is one who acknowledges the fact that the person who designed the grill has a better idea of how to put it together than anybody else! It was a nightmare.) I guess I finally gave in and used the manual after a few hours of putting it together and then having to take it apart because it didn't work properly.

The One who made us has a plan for how to live our lives. He gave us absolutes to live by for our own good, not because he's a killjoy with a lot of rules. Only an idiot would try to put life together without using the manufacturer's manual.

Our children need to be able to watch us live in such a way that there is the least amount of confusion. They need to see us live and make decisions by a philosophy of life that helps us live so consistently that their little eyes don't miss what we're doing and why. Children don't hear us with their ears. Children hear us with their eyes. Whether we like it or not, thought through or not, we will pass on to our children our own personal philosophy of life. Can it be anything less than the instructions to live by that the Manufacturer has supplied? If we settle for less, their lives won't work properly. Happiness will elude them. When they are adults, decisions will be difficult for them to make. The right decisions, that is. Decisions that, later on in life they will be glad they made.

As he tells his story, Brent Sr. pulled over to the side of the road on Interstate 95 and got out of the car. He went around to the other side and asked his son to get out of the car. He then reached in and disconnected the radar detector. Dropping it on the pavement, to the shock of his son, he finished the job by smashing it with the heel of his shoe. Then Brent Sr. looked at Brent Jr. and said, "I'm sorry for setting such a bad example. Will you forgive me, son?"

After that, father and son hugged each other. Do you think that boy will ever forget that moment? The radar detector wasn't something that was against the law, and Brent wasn't even breaking any rules by using it. But it was against a father's philosophy of life. It ran against the lessons for life a father was trying to teach to his son. The day a dad smashed a radar detector and asked a son for forgiveness was the day a son will remember for a lifetime. Right is right and wrong is wrong, regardless of what a society might say. This is part of a philosophy of life that's worth living for. It's a philosophy of life that is worth teaching.

IS IT REALLY THAT IMPORTANT?

When the company sends my son away on a business trip and many other men are participating in activities that are contrary to his wedding vows, will his philosophy of life be important? When my daughter's marriage hits those difficult years, as every marriage does, will her philosophy of life be important? What helps a young person get through those difficult marriage times? Feelings? It must be a faith in something bigger than feelings. A faith that consistently gives answers to life's difficult decisions. When the company offers my son an opportunity for a transfer that will enhance his career but put a strain on his family, how will he make that difficult decision? These are adult dilemmas that require adult decision-making skills. Decisions that will impact the rest of their lives. Are we teaching our child the way to make those mature adult decisions?

Philosophy of life will be the ruling factor in everything my children do when they grow up. It's of the utmost importance that I, as a parent, have supplied them with the opportunity to learn the all-important template to put over all of life's decisions. That way, later on, we'll both be able to say we're glad we did.

THEY ARE DEFINITELY WATCHING US

One night when Robey was about four years old, he was sitting on my lap facing me. With his little thumb and forefinger he reached up to the top of my nose and ran it down both sides of my nose. Immediately, with the same two fingers he ran them down the sides of his own little nose. Robey repeated this very deliberate process several times until finally I asked him, "Robey, what are you doing?" Robey looked my right in the eye and said, "You have grease on your nose Daddy, and I want to have grease on my nose just like you."

I laughed and tickled him for a moment, but later on that night I began thinking about that incident. How closely he must have been observing me to make an observation like that. More amazing was the length he was willing to go to be just like me. Soberly, I wondered, Am I living a life that is worthy of his observation and emulation?

SUMMARY

1. Our society lives by a philosophy of life that espouses "If it feels good, do it."
2. Each parent must think through the question: "What philosophy of life are we teaching our own children to live by?"
3. Our children need a philosophy of life that will give them a constant for the decision making they will face in adulthood.
4. A parent needs to think through and live out that philosophy of life so the child can see the example.

QUESTIONS

1. What do you think your child would say is your priority of life?
2. Does your child know that you have a template by which you make decisions? Is it more than "everybody else is doing it," or does your child know that that's a good rationale to use when he is asking you if he can do something?
3. When analyzing yourself, what do you see as the ruling factor in your life's decisions? Who do you play life's games for?
4. Are there any "radar detector" inconsistencies in your life?

RESOURCES

Josh McDowell & Bob Hostetler; *Right From Wrong* (Dallas: Word, 1994).

Chapter Sixteen

------◄◦►------

Teach the Standard

I know I need to teach my children about how to follow Christ in their everyday walk," one father admitted. "But I don't even know where to begin. I wasn't raised in a Christian home. I mean, I grew up in a churchgoing home, but that was about it. As far as teaching my children how to make Christian decisions, how to make God their priority of life, that's just something I don't really know how to do." And then this somewhat discouraged dad asked the key question, "Where do I begin?"

The first step is to realize the magnitude of this need in every child's life. This dad had already passed step number one. The second step is to understand that it's not the church's job to be the primary teacher of a child's philosophy of life. That job belongs to the parent (Deuteronomy 6). The families of long ago referred to the father as the "provider." But that reference was not such a simple, shortsighted task as parents see today. It didn't mean simply to provide for the child's financial needs. "Provider" meant to provide for the for all the needs of the child, most significantly the child's need to be developing a relationship with his or her heavenly creator. The parent of the past knew it was of the utmost importance to provide the child with ongoing biblical training—in the home. Many discerning parents of yesterday even brought the family Bible to the dinner table to read a passage for discussion and training during the meal. The dinner table and the "training table" were one and the same.

Today's parent has often been deceived into believing that this training is the responsibility of the church. "I sure wish our church would hire a good youth minister so that our children would get the training they need," one parent requested. Taking a child to church and letting someone else train him or her will only give a child the church's philosophy of life. That does not mean it's the same philosophy of life the child observes being lived out by a parent. The youth pastor might be teaching one thing and without realizing it, the parents are teaching a totally different philosophy of life. If the two philosophies conflict, the child will live in a state of confusion and internal unrest. Parents need to see that the child will watch and learn from them far more than from the three or more different youth leaders that pass through their lives.

> *Taking a child to church and letting someone else train him or her will only give a child the church's philosophy of life.*

"I learned an interesting lesson from my parents," one young adult commented. "We would sit in church and my dad was all ears to what the pastor would preach. As we got up to leave my dad might even say something like 'That's certainly a beautiful hat you have on today, Mrs. Smith.' Then as we walked to the door, 'Pastor, that was a wonderful message. It sure blessed my heart. Thank you.'

"I'd walk out of church kind of invigorated just listening to my dad. Then we'd get to the car and once the doors were closed and the engine was started, something would happen. My dad might look at my mom and say, 'Could you believe that ridiculous hat Gladys Smith had on today? And you know what, honey? That's the second time he's preached that message. Look, I wrote down the date in my Bible the last time he preached it. We don't pay him for repeats.'

"I'd sit in the back seat trying to figure it all out," this young man continued. "Actually, I finally learned that the Christian life (philosophy of life) is only for when you're at church. Once you leave the property you go back to acting any way you want to. I learned that by watching my dad."

I LEARNED BY WATCHING

That young man was exactly right. We don't learn by going anywhere. Children and teenagers learn a philosophy of life at home, and it starts by watching their parents. Where does a parent begin? By setting an example.

If the parents' philosophy of life is their faith, what do they do to grow or enhance that faith? How do the parents "feed" their philosophy of life? Does the child see the parents spending any time personally growing that faith? We must decide that this philosophy of life is so important that we will give it the amount of time it deserves each day.

Question: Do I spend as much time reading and studying God's manual as I do reading the paper each day? After all, if this really is the core of my life, shouldn't I spend time every day developing my relationship with God? Which reading will offer me more direction? It depends on what my philosophy of life really is.

One of our tendencies when reading a chapter like this, is to read it on behalf of someone else. "I sure wish my spouse was reading his," one person might think. "This is something she really needs to be doing!" Don't read this chapter for anyone else. Don't even think about anyone else as you consider what steps you may need to take in bringing your philosophy of life to the surface of everyday living. Just focus on your behavior and attitudes. That's all you can do. In fact, maintaining your own philosophy of life is a full-time job. You can't do it for yourself and wish it on someone else too.

A friend of mine accepted Christ as his Savior almost two decades ago. He also decided to make the Christian life his philosophy of life. He realized that his faith could not just be an additive to his life. To make it a priority, he got up early every morning to read his life-management manual (the Bible) and study with a Bible commentary. As a physician, he took on this life-management project in a very scientific manner.

My friend's son woke up every morning knowing that his dad was in the family room having his "devotions." When the son was very little, he would wake up early so he could drag his pillow and blanket into the family room and lie down on the couch near his dad. Today that boy is off in another state, going to college. One of the reassuring, stabilizing factors in his life is the knowledge that each morning his dad is still sitting on that couch having devotions and praying for him. That is one constant this young man has come to count on. His dad was setting an example for how to live and grow in his philosophy of life.

PHILOSOPHY OF LIFE IS CORRECTIVE

There are times when one's philosophy of life offers an opportunity for correction and new direction of the parent. We had just finished our family devotions and it was time to drive to school. The topic of that morning's devotions concerned our responsibility to forgive others when they sin against us. Ten minutes after leading these devotions and pontificating on how important this concept of forgiveness is, I was at the steering wheel driving the children to school. I pulled out onto a four-lane road, and after only a mile or so I was run off the road by another car speeding by. Driving wildly in the weeds, I managed to get control of the car and pull back onto the road. Then came my opportunity to put the pedal to the floor and do whatever it took to catch up to that car and express my anger to its driver.

Robey was sitting in the front seat during this "opportunity" and Torrey was in the back. I was completely immersed in my burst of revenge, but my children were focused on me. They were, in fact, very interested in watching my reaction. I looked over at Robey, who was sitting next to me, just staring at me as if to say, "Dad, how could you so quickly forget the devotions you just taught us fifteen minutes ago?" All of a sudden we all burst out laughing. (Well, not Torrey. She was petrified by the fact that I was so out of control, as well as just plain disgusted with the whole event!) It's easier to teach than it is to live. But it's my living that does much of the teaching. My example of how I live is far more important than anything else I try to teach. *Teaching* my children a philosophy of life starts with *modeling* a philosophy of life.

EXPOSURE TO A PHILOSOPHY OF LIFE

Children will learn much by watching our example, but they also need to be brought into the process. Creating a specific time for family devotions to take place each day will start them into the process of learning about God. It will also introduce them to God, so that they can eventually develop a personal relationship with him.

How Young Can You Start?

Not knowing the exact age to begin family devotions with children should not cause us to wait longer than necessary. The only way to meet that criteria is to start early. In our family, we started reading a family devotional book with our children before their second birthday. That way they will never be able to remember a time in their lives when we weren't having devotions as a family. If a family has older children and they haven't yet begun having family devotions, that's okay. Start today!

It's never too late to begin a time of reading a Bible passage or reading out of a daily devotional book.

It's never too late to begin this time of reading a Bible passage or reading out of a daily devotional book. The majority of the children who come to live at the homes of Sheridan House for Boys and Girls have never been involved in family devotions before they arrive. They range in age from twelve years old to fourteen. Even though these children have never before been involved in this short study time each morning, we still make it a part of their day once they come to live with us. It's never too late to begin.

Procedures for Beginning Family Devotions

Start by going to a local Christian bookstore and ask for help in picking out a devotional guide for your children. There are dozens of options available for parents today, and these options will vary according to the age of the child. Select a book that is focused toward the middle of the children's ages. If a parent has three children ages four, eight, and twelve years old, a devotional focusing on the eight-year-old will be appropriate. The four-year-old will be challenged to stretch and learn, while the twelve-year-old will be able to totally understand what is being taught. Even adults often like the children's sermons in church better than the regular sermon. It's nice to hear something that we can totally understand. Plus the older child is going to be challenged to start having his own personal devotions in addition to this family time together.

Select the Right Time

For our family, the morning hour has been the best time for family devotions. We have chosen to wake up a little earlier than other families do. That way we are allowing ourselves time to sit together at the breakfast table and spend an extra ten minutes having family devotions. Other families might find that another time would be better. Many families have chosen to have family devotions around the dinner table or in the living room before the youngest child goes to bed. The key to making this choice is not what time but rather the right time. The exact time that a family will be able to consistently commit to this discipline will vary from family to family. Select the time that's best for you.

Once you have thought about and selected the time that you think will be the least interrupted, watch the interruptions take place! It's just astounding how a specific time slot that was previously devoid of phone calls or other interruptions will become a busy time. This time will need to be set aside and plans will need to be made to see to it that it is not destroyed by interference from the outside. This is a discipline that will build a relationship and philosophy into a child's life. It needs to be considered one of the most important things a family will do each day. We can't be lackadaisical about it and expect the children to take it seriously.

> *Once you have thought about and selected the time that you think will be the least interrupted, watch the interruptions take place!*

Dive In

There's no easy way to begin the actual process other than to make the announcement that "tomorrow morning we are going to spend an extra ten minutes at the breakfast table reading a passage from this book about the Bible." When tomorrow morning arrives, the parent reading needs to get enthusiastic about this whole process. Read the passage, discuss it a little, ask if anyone has any thoughts or questions, and pray. Ask the family if anyone has any prayer requests. Some families even write these requests down, keeping family prayer journals. It's a great encouragement to list prayer requests and periodically check them to see if there have been answers. Then ask someone to close in prayer. This is an opportunity to teach the children how to pray out loud, as well as teach them how to share each other's burdens through prayer.

Feedback

Be prepared to get excited about having devotions even if you seem to be the only one who is excited. Chances are the children will not stand up and cheer at the end of each reading. Never have I finished reading devotions at the breakfast table and had one of my children stand up and shout, "Wow! That was awesome, Dad! Could we do another one this morning? These devotions are sure going to impact my life today in school." Children are probably not going to cheer over the devotion times, but that doesn't mean that their lives aren't being positively affected. The impact will be lived out rather than shouted about. Our task is the long-term process of helping them adopt a philosophy of life that they will be able to carry with them on into adulthood and beyond. This core belief will take years to be realized.

Be prepared to get excited about having devotions even if you seem to be the only one who is excited. Chances are the children will not stand up and cheer at the end of each reading.

Don't conduct family devotions in order to get feedback from the children. Do it because it's the right thing to do. Do it because the children need a philosophy of life and this is the way to give it to them. Do it because the One who made them and gave them to you said, "Train a child in the way he should go, and when he is old he will not turn from it" (Proverbs 22:6). Teach your children about God because the book of Deuteronomy says to impress these lessons upon the children while they are with you (6:7). The only way to leave an impression is to teach it on a daily basis.

TEACHABLE MOMENTS

One of the greatest opportunities for teaching a philosophy of life is during unscheduled moments when something has happened or a question has been asked. Often these events will happen when it is inconvenient to talk about them. Other times children will ask questions when you least expect them. Some of the most valuable training times with our children have been the unplanned spontaneous conversations that have taken place in the car or while sitting at their bedside. Parents need to be sensitive to those opportunities when children ask those special questions. Questions they might not see as having spiritual answers, but we know are really opportunities to teach a truth. Putting away laundry or getting back to a television program can wait, but that particular teachable moment cannot. Take advantage of the moment so that later you can say you're glad you did.

A PERSONAL TIME OF DEVOTIONS

As the children become teenagers they can add a dimension of growth in their philosophy of life. Having seen their parents have a personal time of devotions or study each day, hopefully, teens will see this is as an adult thing to do. The next purchase is a devotional guide directed at the teen's level. It will need to be interactive with space for them to respond to thoughts and questions and write things down.

The teen should participate in the purchase of this devotional guide by going with the parent to the Christian bookstore to help make the selection. The mere discipline of having devotions each day will be a great lesson for a teen. As a motivator for a twelve- or thirteen-year-old, some parents might want to announce that, though the child's bedtime is 9:30, if he wants to have devotions he can stay up later to do that.

"Carrie, as we pick out this devotional guide for you, I want to say that you can get into bed at 9:30 and instead of turning off the lights, like you usually do, you can spend an extra twenty minutes having devotions instead. You still need to be in bed at 9:30 each night, but whether you need to turn the light off at 9:30 depends on whether you want to have devotions or not. It would be great to see you communicating with God on a daily basis, as each person ought to do. After all, he's the one who made you. It stands to reason that he's the one who has the best plan for you."

Help children set up a personal time of devotions and then lavish them with encouragement about it. "Carrie," a parent might say, stopping by the child's room at night, "I can't tell you how proud it makes me to see you spending this time with God. If I had been this smart when I was your age I certainly would have avoided a lot of problems. I'm proud of you for being so mature."

OTHER HELPFUL MATERIALS

There are many other items available that help reinforce the proper philosophy of life. This generation has an opportunity that no other generation has had. They can choose from over a dozen magazines that are very "high interest" for their age group. These magazines also work at coordinating with parents who are trying to train a philosophy of life that teaches a child about God.

There is also much in non-Christian literature and magazines to be careful of. Many magazines enjoyed by parents themselves just a generation ago are no longer friendly to the Christian philosophy of life. Parents will want to make sure they know what their children are reading. It doesn't make sense for a parent to be attempting to teach one philosophy of life, while the child is receiving in the mail a magazine that espouses the total opposite philosophy. All the time, the parent is paying for that subscription. As a matter of fact, that family will indeed "pay" for the contradiction of having that magazine come into their home.

A PERSONAL TIME OF EXPERIENCE

An important part of the training process is to open up the opportunity for the child and teen to experience God working in their lives. That often happens when the child has the privilege of participating in youth activities such as camps or mission trips with the church group. Then a young person has the opportunity of standing alone, away from home, watching how God is at work around them. The key is to allow them to experience the hand of God in their lives.

As important as these activities are, however, there is no substitute for prayer. Prayer is a great way to open those doors of relationship. In addition to facilitating a daily time of family devotions, children should be prayed with before they go to sleep at night. This is a way to leave them thinking about their relationship with God as they go to sleep. God loves our children more than we do. He certainly desires a relationship with them.

When Torrey was only eight years old she wanted to take piano lessons at her school. It never really occurred to me that in order for my daughter to really benefit from piano lessons, it would be nice to have a piano at home for her to practice on. We didn't have one.

One night while Rosemary was sitting on Torrey's bed praying with her, she asked Torrey if there was anything she wanted to pray about. Our daughter took advantage of this opportunity and asked her mother if we were ever going to have a piano. "I don't know, honey," Rosemary responded. "Let's pray about it, without telling Daddy, and ask God if he will give us a piano." So they did pray about it, and they didn't say a word to me about these prayers.

Just a few days later, I was sitting at my desk at work and I got a phone call from a friend. She said she was in the middle of a move and had an upright piano that she no longer needed. She wanted to know if we wanted it for our kids. I thanked her for the offer and said I really didn't know, but I would call her back tomorrow. That night

I pulled the message out of my pocket and said, "Glenda called today and asked me if we would like her piano." Both Rosemary and little Torrey went into shock. Seeing their shock, I jokingly reassured them that Glenda didn't say I had to carry it on my back, she simply wanted to know if we wanted it. Instantly, I could see that this was no joking matter. Tears were rolling down their faces.

That piano is in our house to this very day. It's much more than a piano, however. That instrument became a symbol to my daughter. A gift from her heavenly Father. Her earthly father might be a fun guy. Her heavenly Father, however, is the king of the universe, one worthy of building a philosophy of life around. He answered her prayer. God did much more than give Torrey a piano. He reached down and gave her a relationship.

Teach your children to pray. It will be a building block in the establishment of their philosophy of life. It's hard to have a relationship without learning how to open up the lines of communication.

STANDING UP FOR ISSUES

This past weekend Torrey and several friends were talking about going to see a movie. The theater had eight movies running simultaneously so there were several choices. Some of the movies that one friend was suggesting were totally inappropriate, and Torrey was concerned about how to handle the situation. Several of her friends wanted to go to the inappropriate movie, and she felt that she was the only one who would be putting up a protest. "What should I say, Dad?" she had asked me.

"You don't have to make a big thing out of it," I responded. "Just tell them that you really don't want to go to that one, but they can go ahead. You'll go to the other movie and meet them afterward."

When we talked initially, I could tell that she was hurting over this incident. The movie she had chosen was the newest Muppet movie. Several of the guys in the group were aggressive football players whom she expected to burst out laughing when they heard which movie she wanted to see.

We talked a little further about the situation and then left the rest up to Torrey. After all, she was seventeen years old and it was time for her to stand up for her philosophy of life. These are times when a parent can become angry at the lack of training that other parents give their kids. But that's wasted energy. These situations are better viewed as opportunities for practice.

Our daughter left for the movies and I sat there hurting for her. Even though I knew in the big picture this was a small event, it seemed big that night. We prayed asking God to give her strength. At 11:00 that night Torrey returned home elated. The kids met

Parents need to make children feel loved, encouraged, and forgiven regardless of the maturity they show.

at the theater and sure enough, she was the only one who didn't want to go to the inappropriate movie. When her friends asked her why, she really couldn't think of a good answer other than "I don't think that's a movie I want to see." That particular answer didn't hold much water with her friends. Feeling alone in this situation, Torrey, quickly said, "That's okay, I'll just go see the new Muppet movie, and you go see that other one. We'll meet when they're over."

As she said that, one of the kids burst out laughing, and Torrey walked over to buy her ticket feeling very isolated. The kids all got in the ticket line, purchased their tickets, and then got popcorn. Torrey laughed with them as best she could and then found out that her best friend had also bought a ticket to the Muppet movie. As the two girls walked toward their particular theater they realized that *everyone* had bought a ticket to the Muppet movie. Torrey was elated. One of the boys was talking about how he couldn't believe they were going to see "this lame baby movie."

As Torrey was excitedly telling us this story, I asked, "What did they think of the movie?"

"It was great, Dad," she responded. "And Jack [the complainer] even thought we should stay and see it again."

As we talked with our daughter that night, it was our job to point out a few things to her. One was the fact that she had done a great job of standing up for what she believed was a decision from her philosophy of life. She had thought through the question "Which movie would Christ want me to see?" We wanted her to know that we were proud of her.

A second thing we wanted her to know was that it was God who had answered this prayer. "If you had not made the decision that you had and taken the stand that you did, this probably wouldn't have happened. But it was the Lord who changed their hearts."

The final discussion pertained to the fact that her job was to stand up for her philosophy of life, regardless of the outcome, leaving the results up to God. "Torrey, remember you prayed for a piano, and then God gave you a piano? Other times you prayed, and for reasons known only to God, you didn't get the answers you wanted. Tonight you stood up for your philosophy of life and everyone followed you. That's reason to be happy. Remember last year when you were involved in that debate on abortion and you took a stand to save pre-born babies? Remember how mad you were at the way so many kids took no stand at all or were even against you? Those results seemed different. But the results are not your business. Your stand is. It won't always work out like it did tonight. But I've got to tell you, we are very proud of the stands you take for your faith!"

Our children need to experience the opportunity of practicing the lifestyle that is consistent with their emerging philosophy of life. The time while they are still with us is the time to let them win as well as get bruised at this endeavor. There will be times when they will not take strong stands. Parents need to make children feel loved, encouraged, and forgiven regardless of the maturity they show. We are encouraging them toward their next opportunity while we are still with them to help them work through the journey. It's a time that requires lots of encouragement from the parents, because peers won't always be so encouraging.

THE FINAL ANCHOR IN ESTABLISHING THE PHILOSOPHY OF LIFE

A philosophy of life that is built around a faith in Jesus Christ starts at the point of making the decision to accept Christ as personal Savior and God. The parents' job is to facilitate that decision. The parents' focus should be on helping the child see the necessity of living life being guided by God, the One who created each of us. This guidance can only be had when a relationship with God is established. But because each of us is a sinner, we cannot have a personal relationship with a holy and just God. As our Father, he breached that great chasm between us by paying the price for sin. The sacrifice for all humankind was made for sin through the death of his Son, Jesus Christ, on the cross. By accepting that sacrifice as payment for our sin, we can have our relationship with God restored.

A philosophy of life that revolves around God's will for my life begins with that first step of dealing with my sin. Christ sacrificed himself to do just that. Accepting Christ is the pivotal step in establishing this philosophy of life. Yes, a faith and confidence in the precepts of the Bible will give my child the right absolutes to live by. But my child will be alone and without God as he attempts to live out that philosophy of life. Lead your child to a relationship with God, through Christ. In our home it was Torrey who led her little brother to a relationship with Christ. It was Torrey who led Robey in a prayer in which he expressed his need for payment for his sin and the acceptance of Jesus as the payment. She didn't lead him to a religion. She didn't lead him to a denomination. Those are only vehicles for worship. Torrey introduced him to the only way to have a relationship with God.

Philosophy of life then comes full circle when our children are able to share that faith with others. A person truly understands what they believe when they are able to share and explain that belief with a friend. Philosophy of life is strengthened when our children have the opportunity to practice living it out. Philosophy of life is impressed upon their hearts when they are taught how to give it out. Teach your children how to share and explain their philosophy of life.

SUMMARY

1. The first step toward teaching a child a philosophy of life is to realize it is the most crucial thing we do as a parent.

2. The second step toward teaching a child a philosophy of life is to understand whose responsibility this training is. It's not the church's responsibility to teach the children about their relationship to Christ. This is the number-one responsibility of every parent.
3. The lessons about philosophy of life begin with parental example.
4. Lead the children in a daily time of devotions as a family and encourage them to have private quiet time as well.
5. Get alone with each child and teach him or her to pray.
6. Help them learn how to stand up for what they believe.
7. Encourage them to share their faith with others.
8. Start by leading them to a personal relationship with Christ.

TRAINING FOR SUCCESS

1. What is the best time to set aside each day for you to lead your children in devotions?
2. What are some of the ways that your children can be allowed to practice using their philosophy of life in their own world?
3. Do you encourage your children when you see personal growth in their philosophy of life? How can you do that better?
4. Have your children each made a personal decision to trust Christ?

Chapter Seventeen

——◄○►——

Conflict or Concert?

When Robey was in middle school, he played in the sixth-grade concert band. The final concert at the end of the year was quite an event. For most of these "musicians," this was their first year of learning to play an instrument. It was more of a contest than a concert. Each section in the band seemed as if they were battling for preeminence! The percussion and the woodwind sections were doing their best to be loud enough for second place. The brass section, however, easily took first place for loudest. It was as if these young musicians had been told that the loudest section was the "winner" of the concert. Each child obviously wanted to make sure their individual parent got his money's worth.

As we progressed through those band years, Robey moved up from one band to the next, and the concerts became less a labor of love and more of an opportunity to listen to truly great music. They learned to blend. Each section learned the balance. Even though the brass section might be prone toward dominance when up against the woodwinds, those horns had achieved a level of restraint. In a march they might be responsible for the melody, but in many other pieces they were simply the backup for the woodwinds. The balance was definitely evident.

The balance and restraint necessary in the adult life is very similar. Three sections in this book have discussed three very important areas of the adult life that a child will need to be prepared for. But it will take more than simply preparing the child for his professional life (employment), his personal life (marriage and family), and then his private life (philosophy to live by). Each of these areas will have a very strong pull. The child will need help in the balance of these three important parts of the adult world.

We understand that there are specific times in life when a person's job seems to take up the most time. Yet that fact should not be allowed to determine that the professional life has the priority position in the concert of life. The conflict of professional life, personal life, and private life will be a raging war until one of the three is given the premiere position. Again, even though there will be times when the job will make great time demands, that doesn't mean it holds the top slot.

> *The conflict of professional life, personal life, and private life will be a raging war until one of the three is given the premiere position.*

Many individuals spend a lifetime battling guilt, feeling that they are not managing their life properly and that important considerations are being neglected. That's because they have no life manager. Without placing one of these areas in a priority role, life will boil down to "oiling the squeakiest wheel." The job world and its demands will scream as the bills and debt seem to beg for primary attention. Lacking a sound philosophy of life, a young person can respond by giving his job top billing without giving a thought toward his personal and private lives. The purpose of a career should be to support the family and glorify God. Because much of our society equates the acquisition of things with happiness, however, making the money to acquire those things can easily become the priority. The young adult can get trapped on this employment conveyor belt.

If a young adult allows himself the time to think about his priorities in life, a conflict will rage in his or her heart. "Am I really doing the right thing? Should we both be working so we can buy the bigger house? Everybody else is. But why don't I seem to be happy? Shouldn't I be focusing all my energies on making money? After all, I'm doing this for my family. But how much is enough?"

The question is not whether or not both spouses should be working. The question is *why* they are working. In many cases both spouses want to work. In other cases, however, both spouses are working only to acquire "things" in hopes of acquiring happiness. When there's no guiding thought process or philosophy of life, young adults will react to opportunity rather than plan for eternity. When all is said and done, what will I be glad I did: Buy the boat or save the money and spend more time at home?

LET THEM SEE YOU BLEND

Children of yesterday were able to observe their parents working through the blend of the three key arenas of life. We used to be a culture that was dependent on God for everything. A hundred years ago when someone was sick, prayer was a vital part of the process. When a crop was harvested, thanks was given to God for his provision. God was the center of all that was done. Interestingly, the church and its steeple used to be built in the center of the town. The citizens were proud that their church steeple was the highest point for miles around.

It used to be much easier for children to grow up and learn how to blend life, because they were constantly standing alongside their parents and grandparents. In good times as well as in difficult times, children could see that faith in God was the number-one priority.

Though times might have been harder without all our modern conveniences, with adults working long hours, the child of yesterday knew that his parents were working for the family. The priority wasn't the office or the work on the farm. The work was done solely to make it possible to feed and meet the needs of the family. After faith in God, it was very evident that "family" was in the second priority. This wasn't a thought that needed to be discussed or diagrammed for the next generation. The lifestyles made it very evident.

Perhaps this priority was easier to see in a society where life was often so fragile. Families that could easily lose four or five children as infants were certain to express more freely the value they felt for the other family members they still had around them. That family certainly wouldn't take their loved ones for granted.

There are many children today who are able to see their parents working hard. Unfortunately, many of these children miss out on the opportunity to see their parents think through the balance. Parents don't share this balancing game with their children. That's either because the parents make life's balancing decisions behind closed doors or, more likely, because most parents themselves haven't been taught the balancing act. Parents need to spend time working through this so our children can see it in action.

THE BALANCE IN ACTION

A man who had a great impact on my life is a businessman in my church who is my age. Many years ago my friend Earl was working as a CPA in one of the large national firms. Earl realized that as he rose up the ladder he was going to be placed in a position where he would have to spend almost all his nights away from home. He might not have worded it like this, but he made a decision: "When my kids are older I want to be able to look in the mirror and say 'I'm glad I did,' rather than 'I wish I had.'" Earl began to think about what his options were.

At that particular time a very wealthy developer in south Florida was looking for someone to become the Chief Financial Officer of his holding company. This wealthy man searched throughout south Florida and interviewed dozens of CPAs. Earl was one of the men he called for an interview. Before the interview, Earl realized that this was the ideal time to make decisions about his work schedule. Better to go into the interview with the right understanding, than to have to do a lot of explaining later on.

At the interview Mr. Smith (the multimillionaire developer) asked Earl many questions. At one point in the interview, Earl saw the opportunity to explain to Mr. Smith who he was.

"Mr. Smith," Earl began, a little nervously, "I operate under a personal mission statement. The first priority in life is my faith in Christ. I have committed to try and never to do anything, in business or in private, that will offend God. The second priority is my family. I say this with all respect to you as an employer. My desire is to work from morning to night, but I plan to try to be home at night and on weekends. I'm aware that that is not always possible, but that's my goal. Helping my wife raise my children is very important to me. I need to participate in their lives. My third priority is my job. I will work very hard for my employer. The hours that I am here, I have a strong responsibility to give it my all. Not just for whoever I work for, but also for God. I felt it very important to tell you that these three priorities are at the very root of who I am."

Earl said that when he finished his little speech, Mr. Smith just stared in amazement. "I've interviewed a lot of people," Mr. Smith finally said, breaking the silence. "You're the first who has said anything like that." Then this older businessman abruptly ended the interview by saying, "Thanks. We'll get back to you."

"Don't call us, we'll call you" was what Earl heard in those words. But the nice thing about that interview was the fact that it gave him the opportunity to practice saying what he was trying to practice in his life. He couldn't expect a seasoned businessman like Mr. Smith to understand what he was trying to say. As respectful as Earl tried to sound in his presentation, it must have either sounded arrogant or totally out of touch. Mr. Smith had looked at him with a look that said, "Come back and see me when you arrive in the real world."

Earl went home that night and took advantage of the real purpose for his mission statement. When his family asked him how the interview went, Earl recited for his children his personal mission statement. His family heard and understood that though his job and career were extremely important, they were not priorities over his family. More significantly, Earl was working at filtering everything through this one statement: "What would I do if Jesus were right here, right now?" His priority, even over his family, was his faith in his Lord. This was a very valuable lesson for his children to hear.

Thirty days later, long after Earl had pretty much forgotten his interview with Mr. Smith, he got a phone call. When Earl was told by his secretary that it was Mr. Smith's company on the phone, he picked up the phone knowing that he was going to hear a secretary say that someone else had been hired. Earl was initially surprised to hear Mr. Smith himself on the line. He wanted to have lunch with Earl.

At lunch, Mr. Smith spent time asking Earl about how he had thought through "this personal mission statement." The elderly man was obviously intrigued that anyone even thought they could live like that. Post-depression men like Mr. Smith just worked hard at their jobs and let the rest of life work in around them. At the end of the lunch, Mr. Smith offered Earl the job. Earl was so shocked he had to ask for clarification. They worked together with a great relationship for almost two decades until Mr. Smith passed away. Both were happy with the relationship, because Mr. Smith understood his employee's mission statement for life. It made Earl very trustworthy and very predictable. It made him a great employee, but more importantly it made him a great family man. Most of all, this mission statement made it possible for Earl to feel as if he was able to pursue God's will for his life. With God as his priority relationship, no one would be surprised at the decisions he made at work or at home. Earl was employed by Mr. Smith but he worked for God. That meant he had to work harder than anyone else. Not longer hours, just harder. His children were able to watch him make these decisions, thus preparing them for their adult decisions. Our children need to be able to observe us work on the balance.

You actually do have to look a gift horse in the mouth! It might be a Trojan horse.

Years ago I was talking to an elderly businessman about a man named Joe, whom I was getting to know in my church. Joe worked for the same international company as the elderly businessman did. As we were talking, it became apparent that this businessman I was talking to even had some supervisory responsibilities over Joe. As we talked about my new church friend, it became apparent that my elderly friend didn't approve of him.

"What's the matter, Mr. B.?" I asked. "Is there something wrong with Joe?"

"He's just hard to figure," the man responded. "We've offered him several opportunities for promotion and transfer, but Joe continually turns down the transfers. His reasoning is ridiculous. He says he's happy here in south Florida, his kids love their church, and they are excited about volunteering in the ministry they participate in as a family. Can you imagine that?"

My elderly friend just couldn't identify with the thinking process that Joe was using. Joe actually brought his kids into the decision making. As a family, they talked about it and even visited one transfer location together. Then after praying, Joe weighed the input of his kids and with his wife made the decision to stay where he was until his kids graduated from high school. He taught his kids about the importance of looking to God rather than "opportunity." One of his statements to his kids was "You actually *do* have to look a gift horse in the mouth! It might be a Trojan horse."

By bringing his children into the decision making, he wasn't showing weakness as a leader. Instead, he was showing wisdom. He was preparing his children for the decision-making process they would face one day. Joe was giving them a time of practice without having to carry the weight of the responsibility of the final decision. This was very wise leadership.

The priority step that we want to teach our children is to live life to be pleasing to God. Many parents might be doing this, but their kids don't see the process. It's important to walk through it as much as possible with the children.

Several years ago it became apparent that I was going to be doing more public speaking than I had anticipated. I would work during the day and speak several nights a week as well as weekends. I was telling people to spend time at home, but I wasn't doing it myself. With the help of my wife, I began to look at my calendar and take control of my schedule before my schedule took control of me. We made two decisions concerning the speaking schedule. One was that I would only speak away from home on Friday nights and Saturday mornings. That way I could be home Saturday night. Further, we decided that I would try to do this every other weekend rather than every weekend. I would no longer respond to the statement, "Bob! We really need you here for this conference." Those statements really got to my ego. My needy ego took over, and I allowed myself to be controlled by "we need you," instead of taking personal control of my calendar.

The second step we took was a little harder for me. I decided that on days when I would be going back out of the house to speak at night, I would either pick up my kids from school that afternoon or be home before they got home. In other words, if I was going to be away from home in the evening, I wouldn't be away in the afternoon. It sounded good, but it was very hard. It wasn't the scheduling that was hard. It was just hard on my masculine ego. There I was at home at 3:00 in the afternoon. Do real men do this? I felt like a slacker. I also felt funny being the only male in the car pool line at school, picking up the children! I know it sounds ridiculous, but I had to get over this. I had to do one of three things. I could wear a disguise when I picked up the kids (but then they still would recognize my car). Since that option wasn't really practical, I thought maybe I could attach a big sign to the roof of my car that said, "I am working tonight!"

I settled on the third option. I needed to decide who I was here to please. God was holding me accountable to train my kids, rather than just pay for them. He was also holding me accountable to teach them how to be adults themselves, by setting an example.

I got very religious about this process for scheduling myself. I planned it all out in my daily planner. I was blessed the day I found each of my children planning out their time with their own planners. The day I saw these results was the day I had the courage to pick them up at school without wearing the glasses with the big nose and mustache (only kidding)!

YOUR FATHER-IN-LAW IS WATCHING

Making decisions about the way we handle our jobs and time away from home seems a little easier than making God a priority over our families. It's only difficult until we realize that God wants us to be sacrificial toward our families. He doesn't want us to abandon our families and be away in church every night of the week. In fact, he sees us as responsible for leadership in our "family church" and membership in the larger community church. We are to act toward our families as if we knew that God was always there watching us, since he really is!

That means adopting a consistent plan for raising my children. That means "training them in the way they should go" (Proverbs 22:6). That also means that I need to handle my marital relationship in a way that would be pleasing to God. If it's pleasing to God, it will be very instructive for the children.

Years ago another counselor in town made a statement to me that I will never forget. It seems so simple, but it adds such a dimension of accountability to the marriage relationship. He said, "Bob, I have just realized that God is not only my father, he is also my father-in-law!"

Well, I'm a different person when my father-in-law is around. I "husband" in such a way that he would leave our home feeling like I'm doing a great job of taking care of his daughter. Several years ago I had one of those great father-in-law show-off opportunities. It was a Thursday when my in-laws were in town to take care of the children while Rosemary and I were going to speak that Friday night. Earlier that day I had lunch with Jim, a close friend. Jim is one of the largest cut-flower importers in the world. As we left for lunch he asked me if I would like to take some roses home to my wife. I would always be delighted to do that, but knowing my in-laws were in town made it all the sweeter.

Jim asked for the keys to my van and he gave them to one of his employees as we went out the door to have lunch. After lunch, my keys were waiting for me in the lobby of his building. When I got in the van to drive home I could smell the scent of roses coming from the back. As I pulled into the driveway I noticed that Rosemary's parents had already arrived. Getting out of my van, I opened up the back to get the roses and experienced the surprise of my life. On the floor of the back of my van was a crate of one thousand long-stemmed roses. I couldn't believe it.

My first thought was, "Isn't God good. Not only all these roses, but on the very afternoon that Rosemary's parents are here. Am I looking great here, or what?"

I opened the box and found the roses wrapped in bundles of thirty-six, so I took them in one bundle at a time. Rosemary's dad was amazed. Rosemary, on the other hand, said, "You must have had lunch with Jim today." She ruined it all. Only after the effect had taken hold did I distribute the flowers to others.

As much fun as I had showing off for my in-laws, I needed to realize that my ultimate in-law is always watching how I take care of and respond to his daughter, my wife. I also need to realize that there are little eyes watching me to learn how to do it. How else will they learn if we don't teach them? My Father-in-law is always watching and he's counting on me to set the example.

NO SEE-SAWS ANYMORE

Have you noticed that the newer playgrounds don't have see-saws anymore? That's because they're hard for children to manage. They require a lot of balance. If a child scoots just a little bit forward or backward on one, the balance can be thrown off and so can his part-ner! When I was about ten years old, my younger brother had a birthday party at a park. There was a see-saw there, and two kids were playing on it. All of a sudden, as a child was walking under the see-saw, the child on the other side of the see-saw jumped off, and the see-saw came crashing down. It barely missed the head of the child who was walking underneath.

Seeing that, I thought my dad was going to make the see-saws off limits. But he didn't. Instead he had me sit in the middle of the see-saw. Then he said to me, "These children aren't heavy enough to be able to keep the balance on this see-saw, so it's not working. All they're doing is fighting to see who can make who stay up in the air. You sit in the middle and move your weight from side to side so the see-saw is balanced." It worked. Sitting in the middle I could decide which end went up in the air and for how long. It made the see-saw a toy rather than a battle scene.

Relating the see-saw to life, the question is, who is in the mid-dle of all the important decisions you make? Who is in the middle of these important areas of life adults are responsible to balance? The professional life can't be in the middle, or everything else will suffer. The worker will never be home if work is the first priority. Under that standard, the more work the better. One end of the see-saw will always be up in the air, so it won't work.

Family is a very worthy priority, but my family can't decipher the important things of life for me, things such as how to live my life, what I am supposed to do with my life, and how to discern right from wrong when they're not around. If family takes priority, the see-saw will still be tilted. Yes, family needs to be a higher priority than work, but family will never have all the answers I will need for life. Something needs to be sitting in the middle, taking priority and helping in the balance of life.

That something has to be my faith in God. The One who made me and knows best for me. The One who has defined right from wrong. The One who is always with me (even as a father-in law). The One who understands the balance.

HOW DO YOU KEEP GOD FIRST?

Keeping God as the priority of your life is difficult. But it can be made easier by following the same two basic principles that Robey's concert band had to learn to do. They had to learn to read the music and keep their eyes on the conductor. Even though they all had separate parts they still had to do these two things.

Learning the sheet music of life boils down to learning how to read the instructions that we've been given. The Creator's sheet music—the Bible. As we read it, we need to teach our children to do the same.

All the time, however, we need to be developing such a relationship with our Father that we think in terms of doing things and deciding about things as if we are in his presence (which we are). We need to not only read the music but keep our eyes and our awareness on the Conductor as we make decisions in our day-to-day lives.

We need to be developing such a relationship with our Father that we think in terms of doing things and deciding about things as if we are in his presence (which we are).

Robey once asked me how I could always know what's right to do. I answered the best I could by saying, "Robey, I want to keep studying God's Word so I can know what's right to do. But I want to live as if he's always with me, so that I do what's right to do." Study the music, and keep your eyes on the Conductor. That way you will be able to keep the balance in the concert. That way the little eyes that are watching you will learn how to do the same. That way you'll be able to say, "I'm glad I did!"

SUMMARY

1. Life for our children will either be a battle of life's priorities or it will be a concert of blending priorities. A lot depends on how we train them.
2. My children need more than the knowledge of the three priority areas of life. And they will need to know more than how to handle their professional life, their personal life, and their private life. They will need to know how these areas of life fit together.
3. The best way to teach my children is to let them watch me work these areas out in my life.
4. The concert of life will boil down to studying the sheet music and watching the Conductor.

QUESTIONS

1. Do your children understand your priorities of life?
2. Have you taken advantage of an opportunity to share with them how you made a decision concerning an opportunity that was offered you?
3. If you were to observe your family, what would you say your children thought of as the most important thing in your life? "The thing that is most important in my dad's/mom's life is_____."

Chapter Eighteen

◄◦►

Most Likely to Succeed

S on," my dad would say, "do you want to live in a house like this?" He'd make that statement while he reviewed my report card. Throughout a couple of my high school years, he was dismayed at my lack of effort. To motivate me, he'd try to point my eyes at a goal—the house we lived in. To Dad, a child during the Depression, success was defined as becoming financially independent. Like many businessmen his age, he put in fourteen-hour days to amass his "fortune." The house we lived in was part of the payoff for his hard work, a symbol of his independence, his success.

I was headed for a tent.

Then one day my dad was forced to reassess what really counted in life. My mother died of cancer in 1964, when I was sixteen years old. Suddenly, the wealth that had been his primary focus provided my father no comfort, no peace. His business, where he had overcome so many other problems of life, was of no help in coping with this tragedy. We were a family in pain, yet not a family. We were unable to help even each other.

YOUR GOD AND YOU DEFINE YOUR SUCCESS

American parents today have all but named education as the god of our children's future. Phrases such as "Get a good education and the doors will open!" "Get a good education and you'll be able to call your own shots!" "Get the right education and you'll be able to live in any neighborhood you desire."

American parents today have all but named education as the god of our children's future.

<o>

Is that success? Following that logic, the real purpose of education is to enable a person to make money. Making money is equated with success.

If money is your benchmark of success, you can forget the need for an education. You don't need an education to make money. Anybody can go downtown on a weekend and sell drugs and make a fortune. Anybody can be successful—financially—by selling drugs.

Or your child could achieve something far more important, at least to a teen. A few years ago several high school seniors from upper-class homes all had the most important symbol of success to a teenager—a snazzy sports car to drive to school. These teens were working at a mall in south Florida. Or so they told their parents, all professionals, who were very involved in their own careers and didn't bother to find out just what their daughters were doing to earn the money to pay for those expensive cars.

Until it was too late. Their daughters were arrested and charged with running and participating in a high school prostitution ring. Although they were successful at making money, they didn't know right from wrong. The money had given them the image of success and momentary pleasure in what it could buy for them, but at a terrible cost. Their proud parents were no longer proud; they were devastated. And these young women had to face the damage they had done that now tainted their entire future.

What is success? Obviously more than just making money. We must also consider *how* we make our money. And what we do with it.

Until a parent can properly define the word *success* for a child, giving clear examples of what is true success and what is false, parenting will be focused only on the here and now; on playing soccer or taking music lessons. Without providing a good example of success, parents fail in that most important lesson that every child must learn—how to take responsibility for your own future, your own actions, and either reap the rewards or pay the consequences.

ANOTHER "SUCCESS"

Sometimes what looks like success and happiness isn't. Several years ago, Nathan, a wealthy businessman, gave me a view of an emptiness that money couldn't fill. "I don't know what's wrong with me," he said. "People think of me as successful. I was even introduced at a dinner the other night as one of the most successful men in the city, and yet I've lost my family and have this ongoing emptiness inside."

To overcome the feeling, Nathan said he would work harder or he'd buy a new car or a new boat. None of it helped. Sitting in my office that day, Nathan was trying to make sense out of his life, trying to find out what had gone wrong and how he could fix it. Nathan had finally reached the point where he realized that although he had made a lot of money, he hadn't been successful. Not successful at life anyway. Divorced from his wife and alienated from his children, an alienation he had never been able to overcome, Nathan now was asking if there might be another reason for life, a reason other than making money.

Once again, it boils down to the definition of success. Is success being one of the best in your field? Freddie Prinze succeeded in a television career, in *Chico and the Man,* a series that brought him fame and fortune. A bright future lay before him when he killed himself at the age of twenty-three. Marilyn Monroe hit the top only to be disenchanted by life.

Despite their "success," we certainly wouldn't define them as successful. Being one of the best is a narrow definition of success. True success is much more than just being one of the best at a particular career. That doesn't cover the broader view that includes happiness and contentment, a feeling of satisfaction.

SUCCESS

One night Torrey and I were working on one of her term papers. We were using my computer. All of a sudden Torrey put the cursor on a small icon of a magnifying glass and clicked it.

"What are you doing?" I asked her, almost in horror. I had no idea what that little magnifying glass with a page behind it was for. I had never used it.

> *We need to teach our children how to gain a better perspective on their life, how to step back from the crisis of today to view the consequences that their decisions have on tomorrow.*

"You said we should print it out so that we could see what the spacing looks like," she explained. "This icon shrinks it down on the screen and we can see the whole page at once. We can see the spacing on the page without printing."

As I looked back at the screen, I saw that she was right. I was amazed. All those years of using my computer I had never known the purpose of the "print preview" icon. I didn't know that I could quickly get an overview of what I was doing.

Sound ridiculous? That's the way many people live their lives. They don't step back to get an overview of their life. They don't consider where they're heading. They deal only with what is right in front of them.

We need to teach our children how to gain a better perspective on their life, how to step back from the crisis of today to view the consequences that their decisions have on tomorrow. We need to teach them how to work at a job so they can take care of themselves. We need to teach them how to pick a mate and then build a life together in marriage. We need to teach them about having a family and providing the physical necessities for their children as well as the emotional building blocks. We need to teach them that each one of us is created for a purpose.

That little icon was put there on my computer screen for a purpose. God has created each person for a purpose. It's the job of each one of us to find out just what God's purpose for us is.

LABELS OF PURPOSELESS LIVES

Each decade has its own label for a lack of happiness or purpose. One decade it was "anxiety." In another decade, adults were hitting a certain age and suffering from "mid-life crisis." Now we're "victims."

The offices of counselors continue to be full of people who can't find their purpose in life. And without a purpose, life can be very stressful. Happiness eludes us.

The only way to find our purpose in life is to first find the One who made us. Our guide in this life is God and his plan for humankind. Only then can we find our purpose. We owe it to the next generation not to soft-peddle that answer.

The proper question to life's difficulties is not "why?" The "whys" of life elude us because the answers are often beyond our scope. Sometimes there is no answer to "why." The question we should ask is "who?" Is anyone in control? Can anyone help me when I feel lost? Who can I go to for answers when my job is not fulfilling or, even worse, when I'm fired? Who can I go to for answers when my relationships are in trouble or even irreparably damaged? When life becomes a mess, who can help? How do you pick up the pieces or walk away from them and go on?

> *God has set certain principles for life, for family, for work. To be successful we must understand those plans of God.*

Success in life is finding a direction that goes beyond job and relationships. Success is learning to allow the One who made us to guide us. Success is living our relationships by the plans given to us by the One who offered us these relationships to begin with. Success in life is working at a job that makes it possible for us to not only meet the needs of our families but also to give generously for the needs of others. We must be obedient in giving. We need to teach our children, by our example, to tithe and, above that, to give additional offerings. We need to teach our children to worship God, not money.

Education is not to be a god, either, but we can use education to further God's plan. We need to teach the next generation how to use education to help them conform to God's plan for life and prepare them for their life's work.

God has set certain principles for life, for family, for work. To be successful we must understand those plans of God. For our children to be successful, we must teach them to understand God's plan.

A LEASE AGREEMENT

Parenting is like a lease agreement. That's the analogy a car dealer came up with. He had attended one of my parenting seminars the night before. During a break he said, "I thought about it last night and figured it out. To put it into my car-dealer terms, parenting is like a lease agreement. We don't own these children, they're just on loan. God has loaned them to us and we're responsible to take care of them until it's time to turn them back in."

He was right, except for one thing. During this "lease" we are responsible to prepare our children in such a way that they will be better when we return them than when we got them. Like the parable of the talents (Matthew 25), there are investments we need to make in our children so that when the Owner comes for them, they will be prepared. We don't own them. They are his. We're just eighteen-year caretakers.

There's a poem by a writer whose name I don't know that sums up this "loan" beautifully:

To All Parents

"I'll lend you for a little while,
A child of mine," God said.
For you to love the while he lives,
And mourn for when he's dead.
It may be six or seven years,
Or twenty-two or -three,
But will you, 'til I call him back,
Take care of him for Me?
He will bring his charms to gladden you,
And should his way be brief,
You'll have his lovely memories,
As solace for your grief.
I cannot promise he will stay,
Since all from earth return.
But there are lessons taught below,
I want this child to learn.

I looked this wide world over,
In search of teachers true,
And from the throngs that crowd life's lanes
I have selected you.
Now will you give him all your love,
Nor think the labor vain,
Nor hate me when I come to take
This lent child back again.
I fancied that I heard them say,
"Dear Lord, thy will be done."
For all the joys thy child shall bring,
The risk of grief we'll run.
We'll shelter them with tenderness,
We'll love them while we may.
And for the happiness we've known
Forever grateful stay.
But should the angels call for him
Much sooner than we've planned,
We'll brave the bitter grief that comes
And try to understand.

It's our job to prepare our children (these children loaned to us) so that they can find success as adults. It's our job to define the full meaning of success. Once we know what our children need to learn before they roll off that eighteen-year assembly line, it's our job to see that they learn those vital principles of living. It's our job to focus on a training process that helps them to face the future as "most likely to succeed" in adulthood.

With all that in mind, shouldn't we dedicate more time to teaching these lessons than we spend on soccer practice? Then we'll be able to say, "I'm glad I did."

FOR MORE INFORMATION

Dr. Robert and Rosemary Barnes have written other books that will help your family. These books can be purchased or ordered from a bookstore near you.

Single Parenting: A Practical Guide to Walk Your Child into Adulthood
Raising Confident Kids
Who's in Charge Here?: Overcoming Power Struggles with Your Child
You're Not My Daddy: Winning the Heart of Your Stepchild
Rock-Solid Marriage: Building a Permanent Relationship in a Throw-Away World
We Need to Talk: Opening Doors of Communication with Your Mate
Great Sexpectations: Finding Lasting Intimacy in Your Marriage

The Barneses also conduct parenting or marriage seminars all across North America. For more information on the seminars, books, or tapes, please call 1-800-838-1552 or write:

Dr. Robert Barnes
Sheridan House Family Ministries
4200 S.W. 54 Ct.
Ft. Lauderdale, FL 33314

Rock-Solid Marriage
Building a Permanent Relationship in a Throw-Away World

Robert & Rosemary Barnes

From almost-marrieds to newlyweds to long-time couples, here's how to build a great marriage...and how to mend the cracks.

Rock-Solid Marriage helps you build strong foundations for a marriage that lasts. Whether you're considering marriage, are facing marital difficulties, or simply wish to improve your marriage, Dr. Robert and Rosemary Barnes show how you can forge a rich relationship that will stand up to life's tests.

Drawing on years of counseling experience and on their own marriage, the Barneses uncover principles essential for a healthy relationship. With a wealth of real-life illustrations, they help you cross marriage's toughest hurdles to achieve the kind of closeness you've dreamed of.

Rock-Solid Marriage
0-310-20804-1- Softcover

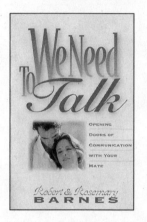

We want to hear from you. Please send your comments about this book to us in care of the address below. Thank you.

ZondervanPublishingHouse
Grand Rapids, Michigan 49530
http://www.zondervan.com